The God of Jacob

Still The God of Reality Today

Samuel D. Hooper

outskirtspress
DENVER, COLORADO

All scriptural references taken from the KJV, NKJV and NIV.

Cover Image by Glenda Krivohlavek

Outskirts Press, Inc.
http://www.outskirtspress.com

ISBN: 978-1-4787-1496-5

Outskirts Press and the "OP" logo are trademarks belonging to Outskirts Press, Inc.

PRINTED IN THE UNITED STATES OF AMERICA

Dedication

The God of Jacob

This book is dedicated to the God of Jacob, known to the world today as Jesus Christ. He has been very much alive in me and through me throughout my life of 80 years. My life has been a life full of trusting in Him. Jesus is my Lord, my Brother, and my Best Friend. He has never left me or let me down. The testimonies in this book are just some of the things He has done for me during my walk with Him. He has simply asked me to put them on paper so that all could know just how wonderful and great He is today. He said, *"Make my deeds known among the people."* So, to Him be all the glory and praise! May you be blessed and encouraged as you read this book. Jesus loves you and wants to be real in your life as well.

--Samuel D. Hooper

Acknowledgements

My appreciation to the Holy Ghost Central church of Alva, TX for the use of their facilities and sound equipment to record the audio CD's from which the manuscript was transcribed. To Pastor Rick Childress for his gracious invitation to do so. I would also like to thank the audio engineers who recorded them for us.

A special thanks to Trinity Fellowship church in Lindale, TX, and their Pastor, Ben Steen, for their financial support and prayers.

Transcribed and edited by Glenda Krivohlavek

Transcription assistant Rhonda Hooper

Co-editor Naomi Horner

Cover text composers Rilda Hooper and Naomi Horner

Cover illustration colored by Jody Krivohlavek

Author's photo taken by Naomi Horner

Contents

Introduction

For sometime now, many people have told me, "You need to put the things that God has done in your life in a book as a testimony that God still walks and works with us today."

I answered, "I'm not a writer, I can't write. I can speak, but I can't write."

Then the Lord began to deal with my heart that He desired for me to put it all in a book to make His deeds known among the people. Why did He cause the Bible to be written? It was for our learning, *"for our admonition, on whom the ends of the world have come"* (1 Cor. 10:11).

I will recount many testimonies in this book and I pray that when you read them your faith will be increased.

"So then faith comes by hearing, and hearing by the Word of God" (Rom. 10:17 NKJV).

Much of God's Word is testimonies of the things that God did in the past. God is no different today. Many people today are tired of religions, whichever one it might be. They're tired of churchianity with no power. They are looking for something real, something that's genuine. Our God is real! People are searching for reality but don't know where to find it or how to contact it, but it's found in Him. True reality is in the One that called us out of darkness into His marvelous light.

The Scripture I felt the Lord showed me to explain the title of this book, "The God of Jacob" is found in Micah 4:1-2 and almost word for word in Isaiah 2:2-3. This is a Word from God and a prophecy for us today.

> *But In the last days it shall come to pass, that the mountain of the house of the Lord shall be established in the top of the mountains, and it shall be exalted above the hills, and people shall flow unto it. And many nations shall come, and say, Come, and let us go up to the mountain of the Lord, and to the house of the God of Jacob; and He will teach us of His ways, and we will walk in His paths;*

This is literally coming to pass in our day. We hear a lot about the prophet, Joel, that said, *"In the last days I will pour out My Spirit upon all flesh"* (Joel 2:28). But this is talking about the last days, as well.

When the Lord began to open this to my heart, I asked, "God, what has 'The God of Jacob' got to do with us today? Jacob lived a long time ago and we are in the New Testament, in the new covenant; we are in the outpouring of the Spirit. What does 'The God of Jacob' have to do with us today?"

I began searching the Scriptures and found many times God is referred to as "The God of Jacob." When most people think about Jacob, they think of him as a supplanter who deceived his father, but God didn't think of him like that. He chose to be called "The God of Jacob," the God who makes Himself a reality to man.

Jacob literally wrestled with the Lord until God granted his petition. The God of Jacob is not just a myth.

He's not just a God up in the heavens somewhere, but He is our God, the God of reality!

The rest of the verse troubled me and I asked the Lord, "What do these mountains and hills represent?"

He revealed to me that they are the organized plans of men which divide and separate the body of Christ. And the "top of the mountain" is the Lord's eternal organized plan for mankind, and that plan is for man to KNOW and FELLOWSHIP with Him!

Today God is establishing the house of the God of Jacob in the top of the mountains and nations are flowing into it and are saying, "Teach us of YOUR WAYS and we will walk in Your paths!"

The God of Jacob is not destroying the mountains or hills; He is just establishing His House above them and inviting people from all nations to flow into His Plan.

I believe that any group, church or person who says, "We want the Holy Ghost to have His way in our lives," is flowing into the plan of God.

The verse says, *"and people shall flow into it."* They're not dragged into it, they are not pushed into it; they flow into it because their heart is after the heart of God.

And they are saying, "Let us go up to the mountain of the Lord, to the house of the God of Jacob, and He will teach us of His ways." Hallelujah! His plan is always the best.

Wouldn't it be wonderful for Jesus to come, sit down and teach us His ways? That would be wonderful, and He can and wants to do just that.

The apostle Paul never sat at the feet of Jesus and listened to Him teach, but when the Lord arrested him, and he spent some time alone with God in the Arabian Desert, he came back preaching the same Gospel as those who had sat at His feet. God can reveal Himself to us in such a way that it would be just as powerful as if Jesus were here teaching us today. When He teaches us His ways, will we then get big-headed because we know more than everybody else? No! We will walk in His ways of humility.

I believe God has some very important assignments for our generation. We can all fit into those assignments if we are seeking after Him. If we are not, He will move on. His plan will be carried out, and we will be left behind! I'm not talking about the "Rapture," I'm talking about the plan of God. He has a great plan for our day, for our generation.

The verse above says, *"In the last days it shall come to pass,"* and God is creating a hunger in hearts to *"know His ways and walk in His paths."* It's hunger that propels us on into the things of God. It is hunger in the natural that draws us to the table to eat. If we're really hungry most anything will taste good. Hunger for God causes people to flow into the plan of God, and God will *"show Himself strong in the behalf of them whose heart is perfect toward Him"* (2 Chr. 16:9).

He has shown Himself strong to the many who have gone from our beautiful country to the countries of the world to proclaim the Gospel. They have gone where the Gospel is not welcome and are being persecuted for their faith in Christ right now. The fact that they are willing to go and be identified as His witnesses in these places is proof that God's plan is on the move.

Jesus told us, *"And this Gospel of the kingdom shall be preached in all the world for a witness unto all nations; and then shall the end come"* (Matt. 24:14).

So if we want Jesus to come quickly, we'd better get busy, because He can't come again until the Gospel (I'm not talking about religion or doctrines) has reached all nations.

I'm not a writer, but I believe the message of this book will bring glory to the Lord. Many of the people who wrote the Word of God weren't writers either, but they wrote as they were moved on by the Holy Ghost. The same Holy Ghost is here enabling this word. I believe the Lord wants people to know that there is reality in serving Jesus, and that He is here with us all the time. So this sharing of my life's experiences with you is for the glory of God. Not any glory to us all glory to Him. We believe that it will be a faith builder to all who desire to have that relationship with God that He wants with us. It is an every day relationship, not just once in a while. He created us for His pleasure. It is hard for us to realize that He takes pleasure in us, but He really does enjoy fellowshipping, talking, walking, and working with us. Praise God! And what a joy it is for us to know The God of Jacob, to be taught of Him and to walk in His ways.

--Samuel D. Hooper

Chapter 1

God's Call

The Early Years

The Lord blessed me to be born into a Christian family. My father and mother were devout Christians. They met and courted in the cotton patch in Texas. Picking cotton was where they began to court. It wasn't just holding hands walking down the street, they were picking cotton; and the Lord joined them together in Holy Matrimony. God called Dad to preach while he was picking cotton. A lot of things happen in the cotton patch. Those of you who have never picked cotton don't know what you've missed. Ha!

I've picked my share of cotton, and I said, "If I ever grow up and be a farmer, I will *not* grow cotton."

The Lord began to deal with my dad, he would see visions while he was picking cotton, of himself speaking to multitudes of people. So he began to see and understand that the Lord was calling him to minister; but as a young man growing up, his eyes were really bad and he could hardly see. He made it through the third grade, which was all the education he had.

He could hardly read or anything; and finally he said, "God, if you want me to preach the Gospel; then You're going to have to heal my eyes and teach me how to read."

"Well," God says, "I guess I had better get somebody else then." Ha!

Is there anything too hard for our God? One day as he was praying and seeking the Lord; he said a funnel of bright light came down all around him and when the light lifted, his eyes were healed! Hallelujah!

Then he began to take his Bible; and every word that was over three letters, he'd have to spell it, and try to read it. And God began to teach him how to read.

One day he was going to a prayer meeting driving his old Willys-Knight. Have you ever heard of a Willys-Knight? Well, that's what he was driving. The Bible just appeared open in his windshield; and he began to read it. He didn't know that what he was reading was in the Bible.

When he got to prayer meeting, he asked, "Is there such a Scripture in the Bible?"

"Oh yes," they answered.

Someone got their Bible, opened it up, and showed him where that Scripture was found in the Bible. From there God began to reveal Himself to him through the Word. He never had a Bible with a concordance, he never read commentaries, but he talked to God, and God just revealed His Word to him. He would take him from Scripture to Scripture, would open his understanding and reveal Truth to him.

Not too long after that the Lord blessed their lives with me. I was a blessing to my family. I was born in Winters, Texas. I'm a genuine Texan. We stopped by Winters, Texas; and there is where I was born.

My parents were so happy; but within a few weeks, the enemy says, "I'd better take him out."

Wouldn't he like to have taken me out then? Wouldn't he like to have taken you out long ago? I had developed double pneumonia and they didn't give me any hope to live.

But my dad and mother laid me on the altar, and said, "Here he is Lord, You gave him to us, but we give him back to you, here he is; give him his health."

God healed me!

The Flat Tire Test

When I was very young, just a few months old, my dad was going out to Arizona to help in some church work in this ol' Willys-Knight. They loaded every little thing they had on that truck and put some gas in the drum and took off. They hadn't gone two miles when they had a flat tire. In those days you had to fix your own tires. You stopped, jacked the car up, took the wheel off, broke down the wheel; you took the tube out, patched the tube, put it back in the tire, pumped it up with a hand pump, and put the tire back on the car. That's the way you fixed flats. So he got the flat fixed; put it on, and went just a few more miles; and another tire went flat. Before he had gone ten miles he had 23 flats! Now let me tell you; when you feel and know that God wants you to do something, that doesn't mean the way is going to be perfectly clear and everything is going to go exactly the way you want it to go; but it does mean that I AM is with you.

So when he fixed the last flat, he got back in the car, and said, "God, if I have another flat; I'm not going on."

He hadn't gone a hundred yards when the next tire went flat!

So he stopped and got out and fixed it; and when he got back in the truck, he asked, "Now what?"

"God, I'm going on anyway," he declared.

They went the rest of the way to Arizona and never had another flat!

The enemy comes to test us, but all he really does is give us a brand new testimony. If we can see that the tests which the enemy brings to get us down, is God's way of propelling us into another realm of faith in Him; it will encourage us, because every testimony is an increase in our faith.

Financial Provision

For several years Dad and Mother journeyed back and forth from Texas to Arizona in ministry. On one occasion they came to a town in New Mexico and they were almost out of money and out of gas.

The Lord spoke to Dad and said, "Go to the Post Office and call for your mail; general delivery."

They were just passing through.

So he found the Post Office, went in, gave the clerk his name, and asked if there was any mail for him.

The clerk searched through the general delivery, "Yeah, here's a letter for you," he said.

He opened the letter that read, "The Lord put it on our hearts to send you $20.00 to this Post Office, general delivery, for your need."

I'm talking about reality. God is still the One in control. He knows right where we are all the time. You think GPS is great? We've got a God better than that. Hallelujah! He knows where we are, and He knows what our needs are.

On another trip he was going along and finances were getting low again. He was walking down the sidewalk and looked down and there was a twenty-dollar bill. It had been walked on so much it was almost completely worn out; and nobody had ever seen it, but there it was! God doesn't do everything the same way every time. But you know what happens to you when those things happen? Oh my; you realize how wonderful God is, and how present He is. He is a present help in every time of need.

For several years Dad went to many out of the way places where other preachers wouldn't go because there wasn't a lot of money in offerings and things like that. By this time he had really stepped up in life. We didn't have the ol' Willys-Knight, now we had a 1931 Packard. He took it, and sawed it half in two, right behind the front seat, and built a truck box that served as a camper on the back. He was a little bit ahead of his time. Now there are pickups with campers. That's where our home was. Our back yard was the white lines of the highway as they flew behind us back there.

In our growing up we never had a home, but yet we had a home. After I was born Mom and Dad had a daughter, and then several years later, another daughter. So I have two sisters and no brothers. We were raised on the highway. Trying to get some education; we would change schools five or six times a year. I was very backward. My mom would travel with you all day in a car and never say a word if you didn't ask her a question. She was very timid and very quiet. She never had to give account of very many idle words when she faced the Lord. (See, Mt.12:36). And so I was timid. You know, we'd go to those schools and have no friends, nobody, and didn't know what the curriculum was in the school, and have to learn all of that. About the time we would learn that and get adjusted, we'd go somewhere else.

People used to really criticize my dad, "You're just dragging your family all over the country," they would say.

"I'm sorry you feel that way, I'm just obeying what God told me to do," he would reply.

All three of their children are whole-heartedly following Jesus. It pays to obey God.

Born Again

I remember a few years later, when I was about seven years old.

We were having an old brush-arbor meeting in the rice fields of Arkansas, and the mosquitoes were so large we called them levee walkers.

Early one morning my dad came by where I was sleeping, and said, "Son, I want you to get up and go pray with me today."

Now, I didn't feel like praying, I was a young boy; and I was asleep. I really didn't feel like getting up to go pray, but when my dad said something that's what he meant. I knew that I'd go pray, or I would get a whipping and then go pray.

"I'd better just go right now," I thought.

So I got up and went with him.

It was between crops, and there was an old empty corn crib out behind the people's house where we were staying. Dad got down on his knees and began to pray. He had one son and he wanted that son to know Jesus.

When he began to pray, conviction came into my heart. Dad was very strict so I didn't know anything about sin. I wasn't a bad sinner but I felt like the worst sinner in the whole world there in the presence of the Lord. I just wept, and wept. The floor was soaking wet around me with tears. From that day until this, the Lord has been very real in my life.

I can remember, as we would be driving sometimes at night and it would be a beautiful moon-lit night and I'd be sitting up front next to the window of this ol' Packard, looking up at the heavens, just worshiping Jesus. Just loving Him and feeling His presence in my life. So I had a rich life.

I believe the God of reality, who my dad knew and wanted his son to know through experience, still wants to be real to us today, no matter what age we are. He still desires Dads to be examples to their children of obedience to the still small voice of God. He wants to convict our hearts of sin so that He can cleanse us from our sins and bring us into sweet fellowship with Him.

Filled with the Spirit

As I became a teenager and we were fellowshipping with different churches, some of the teenagers from the churches wanted to steal gas from the farmers and do things that were not right. I began to realize I needed more than what I had. Even though I had a genuine relationship with the Lord, I needed that power that Jesus said you would get; *"after the Holy Spirit is come upon you"* (Acts 1:8). Personally I needed that, so I began to go to the altar in the church there and pray and seek the Lord.

"I want to be filled with the Holy Spirit," I said, but I made a little stipulation, "God, I want the real thing. I want what they got on the day of Pentecost. God, I'm not seeking tongues, because when I go to a shoe store and buy shoes; tongues just comes with them. I want the real thing. I want the Holy Ghost. I want Your power, Your anointing in my life."

I couldn't seem to get through. I don't know what the hindrance was but I couldn't seem to get through.

I didn't want somebody to say, "I think he got it."

I didn't want anyone to have to tell me if I got it or if I didn't. I wanted the *real* thing. So finally I got desperate. I was about seventeen at the time and we were staying in Imperial Valley in southern California. I was working with a man that was a beekeeper. I asked him if I could have a few days off.

He asked, "Well, why do you want to take off? What do you want to do?"

"I want to go out to the desert, and get filled with the Holy Ghost," I replied.

He said, "Okay, you can go."

He loaned me a little ol' Model A Ford so I could drive out into the desert. It is 180 feet below sea level and the sun is extremely hot.

In fact, my cousin said, "If hell is any hotter than this place, I don't want to go there."

"Well, it sure is," I said.

I told Mom and Dad, "I'm going to the desert. I'm going to seek the Lord. I'm going to be filled with the Holy Spirit. Don't look for me to come back until I'm filled with the Holy Ghost!"

I got in that old car and drove out in the desert. I stopped by an old creek bed that only had water in it when there was a flash flood. I started walking up this dry creek bed; it's just me and Jesus.

"God, here I am," I said. "I am here until my bones bleach in this desert, or You fill me with the Holy Ghost."

I'm telling you, it was like a lightening bolt from heaven! I hardly got the words out of my mouth and the Holy Ghost descended on me and He came to live in me; and He is still living in me. It's real! We can have the real thing. Coca-Cola has as their slogan, "It's the real thing." Well, it's not; the Holy Ghost is the real thing! Hallelujah!

Like I said I was very timid, but that's when I changed. Because when I came to myself, I was jumping straight up and down, I don't know how high; and speaking in languages I'd never spoken before! The tongues came with it; Praise God. Hallelujah!

When I finally got back in that ol' Model A and drove it back home, they took one look at me and said, "He got it, he got it; he got it!"

They knew because my face was shinning. Not quite as bright as Moses' was, but it was sure shinning; and the Lord filled me. Don't settle for imitations. Get it from God direct. When you get it from Him direct, you get the real thing.

Answers to Why

Right after that, I was going with a young lady that really loved Jesus; and God put us together in Holy Matrimony. So when we got married we moved from Imperial Valley up to San Bernardino, California; about 60 miles from Los Angeles. There God blessed me with a good job and we began attending the Muscoy Community Church. It was a full Gospel church but they called it a Community Church. As we often did in those days, we would gather early and pray around the altar before the service began. I don't know where we got away from that practice, but that's a powerful thing to do. One time as my wife and I were kneeling and praying around the altar, some people came over to us. I didn't know them and they didn't know me. They laid hands on me, and began to prophesy.

They said, "Because you've been faithful to go with your parents, and haven't grumbled about the things you had, or didn't have, I am going to bless you and give you everything that you ever wanted."

How about that! Would that be good news? Absolutely!

So listen, when we are tested and tried, that doesn't mean that's the end of it; because there's somebody watching, somebody is taking notice. And one day, watch out; when the blessings start to flow. So let's not murmur or complain, let us be thankful and happy with whatever God provides.

When I was a child growing up I never had any new clothes, they were always hand-me-downs. I had one new pair of shoes in my life; until I got out on my own. Dad was a mechanic and he was always working on people's cars for free, and by doing it that way, you never run out of cars. I would sit in the car sometimes when Dad would go into the parts store to get parts, and watch people in their nice clothes walking down the street and you could tell that they were well blessed.

I would just talk to the Lord, and say, "God, I don't understand, Dad is doing everything you want him to do, he's pouring out his life. He's going to these places and ministering to people and if people don't have a way to church, he picks them up, takes them to church and then takes them back home again. Instead of getting money he's pouring it out. I don't understand why he's doing that, and we don't have anything, and they have all the wealth and riches?"

You know, the Lord never answered me until that night at the altar, but He heard me.

"Because you were faithful and didn't complain and murmur about the things that you didn't have and other people have," He said.

When I was talking to him, I wasn't complaining, I just didn't understand why. The Lord wants us to ask why because He wants to make us to know why.

Sharing the Blessings

The Lord began to fulfill that prophecy. Everything that I touched, God blessed. He blessed me with a good job and we had everything we needed. Within a year's time I had already built a brand new home with a tile roof. Sometime later I was able to buy Mom and Dad a brand new pickup and put a camper on it. They never had anything like that. I was able to help missionaries in other countries. I was just being exceedingly blessed.

We helped Muscoy Community Church go over to another town and start a work there. They wanted an outreach to other communities and other people. I volunteered to go and help, so I was "Youth Director" in that church. God was moving and blessing. We outgrew the building in a very short time and had to start working on a bigger building.

Everybody was giving and we were paying for it just as we went. We didn't take out a big loan, God paid for it. We came to the place where everybody had given until we didn't have any more. We needed more material but we didn't have the money to buy it.

One night a call came for the Pastor.

"Would you please come and pray for me? I'm sick," the lady pleaded.

So the Pastor and his wife got out of bed about two o'clock that morning and went to pray for her.

She said, "Before you pray, let me tell you this; Night before last, God spoke to me and told me to give you a thousand dollars for your church project. 'God; I can't do it,' I replied. I couldn't sleep all night long, and last night I still couldn't sleep. God told me, 'Give them two thousand.' But I said, 'I sure can't afford that!' And I couldn't sleep all night. So tonight I have not been able to sleep. Then God said, 'Give them three thousand!'"

God went up a thousand every night and she still couldn't sleep. How many know; if you can't sleep for three nights it gets pretty bad.

"Please take my check and pray for me," she said.

That was just the amount we needed to buy the material and complete the building. The Lord knows what we need. I'm talking about the God of reality.

God's Unmistakable Call

Now everything was going so good, I mean, so good; God was just blessing and working. I was a plastering contractor and worked in many cities in southern California. One day while on the job all of a sudden, I was caught up in a trance, just caught away; and like Paul says, *"whether in the body, or out of the body, I do not know, God knows"* (2 Cor.12:3 NKJV). But I know what happened to me; the Lord caught me up in this trance. He took me in this plane air ride over my home and my possessions that I thought were so much; and for somebody who never had anything, it was a whole lot.

God showed me all of my earthly possessions, and then asked me, *"Do you love Me more than these?"* (John 21:15 NKJV)

I was in a position that I couldn't say anything; because I had told the Lord, "I'll do anything, just don't ask me to be a preacher. I've had all the traveling I wanted. I've settled down, got my family, got my home, got my job; everything's there, that's all I want."

I knew what He would say if I said, "Yes," because I'd read the

Book; and what He told Peter, *"Feed my sheep"* (John 21:17), that meant--go preach.

So that part of me I had reserved for myself. When we serve God, we can't put a stipulation on our life.

When we say, "God, I'm yours."

He will say, "Son, I'm yours and all I have is yours."

But many times we can't go that far, we don't want to take that step; that total commitment. Especially for things that we don't want to do. Now that's where I was.

I did love the Lord, and I wanted with all my heart to say, "Yes Lord, I love you," but I knew what He would say.

Then I thought, "Well that's really not fair, Lord; You are the one that blessed me with all these material things, and now you want to know if I love You more than them?"

It just didn't seem right. But I couldn't say anything, and the Lord had mercy on me, and whoosh; dropped me back down there on my job.

Months went by, and I hoped that the Lord had forgotten all about that, because it didn't change me. I really didn't want to be a preacher. I'm not going to go into all the details of why I didn't, but I met some that weren't so nice, or so genuine, or weren't so sincere, and the motives of their hearts were not right. I did not even want to be identified as a preacher. I had bitterness in my heart because of preachers who were suppose to be the example to the flock, and they weren't.

I was working along one day; several months later, and the same thing happened to me again.

"Oh no, it's happening again; and I still can't answer!" I thought.

The Lord knows our hearts, but He also knows what He has called us to do. What He has chosen for us to do; His plan for our life, not our plan; His plan. He had to help me that day.

He took me up in that plane air ride again, and showed me our possessions; but this time it was a little bit different, because while I'm trying to figure out what I was going to say; He said, "I'll help you."

He took his hand and turned my head. Looking over to my right was a huge group of people. People that I had never seen, people I didn't know, not my family, just souls; people. When I looked at them they were the saddest looking people I had ever seen. Then I looked up, and Jesus was coming and they were lost! When I saw that, my heart broke, my heart melted, and I realized for the first time how valuable souls are! I was raised in the church by a very strict parent, and I slept on the church benches more than I slept in beds the first part of my life, but I did not know the value of a soul! I realized that when Jesus comes not one earthly thing that I possessed would be worth a snap of your fingers! The only things of value were those souls that I said I didn't want to preach to! Then my heart broke, and I just melted before God, and I wept, and wept.

After that, from the heart, I could say, "Yes Lord, yes I love You more than anything else in this world."

When I said that and I looked back at those people; their hands were lifted, their faces were shining, and they were saying, "Come quickly Lord Jesus!"

I was saved when I was seven, filled with the Spirit at seventeen; but that day I got converted!

I knew then what Jesus meant when He told Peter, *"when thou art converted, strengthen your brethren"* (Luke 22:32).

Did you know Peter's name was already written in "The Book of Life?" Jesus had sent them out, they healed the sick, cleansed the lepers, raised the dead, and came back rejoicing that the devils were subject to them.

"Nevertheless, do not rejoice in this , that the spirits are subject to you; but rather rejoice because your names are written in heaven" (Luke 10:20 NKJV), Jesus told them.

So their names were already written there but they hadn't been converted yet. I believe there's a conversion coming to the "church" when the Lord opens our eyes, and we see how valuable the souls of people are that are lost without Christ. He's coming, and they're lost! All of our new homes, nice cars, businesses, and everything else we have, won't be worth a snap of your fingers; because we're going to be with Him where He has prepared a wonderful place for us. The only things of value on this earth, really; are the souls of people.

From that day till this, it hasn't been, "What's in it for me?"

It is; "Lord, what would You have me to do? How can I win the lost? How can I bring them to You?"

I believe the secret lies in what Jesus said, *"Follow Me, and I will make you fishers of men"* (Matt. 4:19).

The secret of winning souls is following Jesus; letting Him speak through you to touch the hearts and lives of men, women; boys and girls.

His example is, *"Follow Me."*

You know, sometimes people go out soul winning and they've got it all laid out. If that's the way they want to do it, that's alright, but it's not the best way, because no two people are exactly alike. No two people have the same needs and desires. No two people have the same resistance, for whatever reason. So we have to be led by the Holy Spirit, which is the Spirit of Christ, to know what to speak into that person's heart, the thing that will touch their heart; so that they will come to Christ because they choose to come to Christ. We are not forcing a doctrine on them, we're not forcing a religion on them, we're not even forcing Jesus on them; we are presenting Jesus.

Just for example, in one instance; I was standing on the street corner waiting for some people to get something done to their car, when a homeless man came up to me and asked for a handout.

I told him, "You know, we're almost in the same position, because I don't have anything; but my brother is rich."

I started telling him about my brother and how He loved people, had money and was rich.

"Well, I sure would like to meet your brother," he said.

I said, "His name is Jesus," and I led him to Jesus.

Jesus is our brother, so I wasn't deceiving him, but that was the way the Lord caught him on the hook and got him. Magnify the Lord. Just lift up Jesus. Let the Holy Spirit give you what to say when you're talking with somebody.

Now back to my answer as this call came to me from the Lord. He answered my "Yes" exactly how I knew He would.

When I said, "Yes, Lord I love You."

He said, "Feed My sheep."

But he emphasized My sheep. They're not our sheep but they're His sheep. Well when I came back down after that plane air ride this time, I was a very different person.

When Jesus looked into Peter's heart, and said, *"do you love Me more than these?"* (John 21:15 NKJV)

He said, *"Yes, Lord, You know that I love You"* (John 21:15 NKJV).

He repeated it again. Three times Peter denied the Lord; three times Jesus asked him, *"do you love Me more than these?"* Then He said, *"Feed My sheep"* (John 21:15-17 NKJV).

We don't find any record where Peter ever turned back. The Bible doesn't say he never went fishing again, but he didn't go back to the fishing profession. He followed Jesus all the way to the end. He became a strong testimony of the resurrection of Jesus Christ until the day he was killed for that same testimony.

God's Call Confirmed

After I said yes, I began trying to figure out how I could make all the arrangements that must be made to answer the call. My dad and mom came from back east for a visit. I was working in Barstow, California, about 75 miles from San Bernardino, driving up there, working, and coming back every day.

When I got home, Dad said, "Son, they're having a revival meeting in Fontana in an old theater, and I just feel like we ought to go tonight."

"Dad, I'm tired," I replied.

When you work ten and twelve hours a day and drive there and back; you're tired.

"But son, I think we ought to go," he said.

What is honoring our father and our mother, anyway? It's honoring them by loving and respecting them and by doing what they've asked you to do. However, if that parent is not a Christian, and they are trying to get you to do something outside of the will and Word of God, then you have to take a stand. In this case my dad was being led by the Spirit of God.

So I answered, "Okay Dad, if you feel like we need to go, I'll go with you."

I bathed, changed clothes and we all went. When we got there the building was packed. We had to sit about three fourths of the way back on the side of the building.

When they turned the service to the Evangelist, he walked up to the podium and said, "I can't do anything until I obey God here tonight. As I was driving on the freeway from Los Angeles to Fontana, God spoke to me, 'Samuel, Samuel;' and I asked, 'What is this Lord? My name is not Samuel.' The Lord said, 'There is going to be a young man in your service tonight who is named, Samuel.'"

You know, God knows our name!

He looked at me and said, "Samuel, come here."

My heart was racing and the hair on the back of my neck was raising up, because I knew that man didn't know me, and I didn't know him.

So I went up, and he began to speak the thing that God had called me to do. That's powerful---that is powerful! I *knew* it was God; because there wasn't any other way he could have known who I was, or the fact that I was even there.

But see, God moved on my dad to get me there and God told that Evangelist that I was going to be there!

To put it in our own terms, "That's supernatural." That's not natural because there's no way a human could know that. This was God without a doubt. My aunts, uncles, family, and many others were in the service that night. So everyone who heard knew that God had set me apart for His work.

God called me personally, in a private, personal relationship, and now He was calling me publicly. He didn't want any doubt in me or in anyone else that He had chosen me. See, when you're following God, you don't have to walk in doubt and fear and unbelief; God will make it clear! Do you understand? God has a way, and He does things His own way; and He doesn't always do it the same way.

Now I was ready and willing to go proclaim the Gospel.

I don't know how many times I've said, "God, thank you for not letting me have my own way in life because there's no greater joy than leading people to Christ."

I'm telling you, there is no joy that can equal that. When you lead a soul to Jesus, and see God work in their hearts and lives, it is wonderful. Look what I would have deprived myself of. Suppose I'd have kept working and become rich, had a big retirement, and wealthy today; and all those souls that He showed me would be lost.

I'm so glad He didn't let me go my way. I'm glad He gave me the ability to say, "Yes." He helped me; He showed me the value of souls.

Did you know there are many Christians attending churches today that do not know the value of their own soul; much less, the value of other souls? What is the value of your own soul? Jesus said, *"If a man would gain the whole world and loose his soul, what would it profit him?"* (See Matt. 16:26; Mark 8:36). Yet many times people let little things; just little things keep them from coming to Christ. Not the whole world, just little things; that have no value, really. But God, I believe, wants to reveal to us His heart. He sent His Son, His only Son, into the world to seek and to save those who were lost. One time we were lost and Jesus came to seek and to save us. That's the reason He came, and that is still His purpose today.

He said, *"Go out into the highways and hedges, and compel*

them to come in, that my house may be filled" (Luke 14:23).

How can we compel them to come in? It's with the love of Jesus. As His love is spread abroad in our hearts by the Holy Spirit, we will begin to love the souls of people that are eternal. He didn't just die for Americans, but for every single soul all over the world. He loves them. He loves us all.

I began in earnest to get everything ready to go. I put my house up for sale, but it didn't sell.

I told my partner in the construction business, "I will be leaving here pretty soon, because the 'Go ye' has got in me, and I can't stay."

He replied, "Oh no, you can't go; you just *can't* go!"

We were doing really well in our business making a lot of money and everything was going great. My family was also growing, now we had three children.

"You just can't leave," he told me.

"But I'm going to. I don't know what day it'll be, but one of these days; I'm going," I said.

I kept trying to make things work out. I was trying in my own effort to get things ready, so I could get going and do what God had called me to do. But nothing was falling into place. You know, if God is for you, everything goes His way; and if it's not His time, it doesn't go His way. It's like butting your head up against a wall. Every move I would make just found a dead end.

A Prophet Sent

Finally one morning I heard a knock on my door. I answered the door, and there was a brother I knew who was also a prophet. He only had one good leg and used crutches to get around. God sent him all the way from Tulsa, Oklahoma to San Bernardino, California, on a Greyhound bus with a message for me! I'm telling you, God cares.

When the Lord spoke to him to take that message to me; he

didn't say, "But Lord, that's a long way, I can hardly get around, and I don't like riding the bus."

No, he didn't say any of that. He just got his bus ticket and headed out.

"I've got a message from God for you," he told me.

I said, "Give it to me, Brother; give it to me."

I wanted to hear what God said, whatever it was; I just wanted to hear what God had to say.

"The Lord told me to tell you, 'There is a difference between the calling and the sending,'" he said.

This word brought such a rest to my spirit, and also answered a question in my heart that I had been so burdened over for many years, because I had seen young people, young couples; out of zeal, jump up and run to do something for God; or go to the mission field, and they'd come back defeated. And many times they never ever got into the calling that God had given them because they didn't wait to be sent.

"Brother, thank you, thank you; thank you!" I said.

You talk about a peace that came in my heart; just a peace. I made a covenant with the Lord at that time.

I said, "God, I'm going to forget about going, I'll continue to be occupied right here until You tell me to go. When You tell me to go I'll go; no matter what is happening no matter what I'm doing, how much money I'm making, or anything that's going on. I will go when You tell me to go."

I realize now that this is the foundation we need when we go, because when we go we're going to meet the adversary. He will be right there to confront us.

When he asks, "What are you doing out here anyway?"

If we can't say that God sent us, he'll defeat us. But if you can say in your heart, God sent me; he has to back up because he knows that's the truth. When we know the truth and speak the truth; he has to leave.

Moving Day

So I just kept working on my job and in the church. Just occupying and just staying busy for Jesus and on the job. Then I decided to build a brand new home. I picked out a beautiful site in the city of San Bernardino, overlooking the hills in the town; a beautiful area. I put everything in that new home that I had ever seen when I was working on other homes; that I wanted. Every room was designed just like I wanted it, just perfect. We were living in a rented house then, because we did finally sell our house.

When it was all finished I told my wife, "I'm going to go check today in town to see if our house has passed inspection."

Because out there you can't move in until it's passed the final inspection. They come out, they check everything, and when they sign it off; you can move in.

"I really believe that it's been signed off, and today we will be moving in," I said.

You know that is an exciting time, when you've done everything all these months; you've been building and working and put everything into it, and now today is the day you move in!

I was so excited, "Just start packing and getting ready, because today we're going to move in," I told her.

So I went to the inspector's office in town and checked; and sure enough, it had passed inspection. My goodness, you talk about a happy fellow now!

I walked out, got in my car and started driving home to begin moving into our new home!

Then the Lord spoke to me and said, "Don't move in, it's time to go."

Now what was I going to do?

I had already told God, "No matter what's happening, I'll go."

Now He was putting me to the test! Well I'm telling you, I turned around and looked in the back seat and there wasn't anybody there;

but I was hearing from God. There wasn't any ifs, ands, maybes or buts about it; God was talking to me! The hair on the back of my neck was sticking up. His presence was in that car in a powerful way!

This was my answer, "Ok Lord; but how do I tell my wife?"

That was my big hurtle. Giving up everything, I could do that. But how can I tell her because she was so excited to move into the new house?

He wouldn't tell me; and I got a little bit aggravated, and said, "Now wait a minute God, I know You're in this car, You just spoke to me. Now tell me how to tell her."

I was getting anxious because I didn't know how to do that. I really didn't know how to approach her. He wouldn't tell me anything, so I started driving a little slower, to give the Lord a little more time.

I had to have an answer, I was desperate to have an answer; and He wouldn't tell me anything! I finally pulled up in the driveway, parked out by the garage, got out of the car and walked in slowly.

I pleaded, "Now God; please, please give me an answer. I've got to have an answer. What am I going to tell her? How am I going to tell her?"

So I reached the front door, and no answer. It's amazing how God can talk and then shut His mouth and not say anything. I got to the door and the screen was hooked, so I knocked on the door.

She came to the door, real excited, looking chipper; and I thought, "Oh my goodness; Lord, what am I going to do? How am I going to tell her that we are not moving into the new house?"

"Honey, I've got something to tell you," she said.

I thought, "Oh good, that'll give me a little more time; let her talk awhile, because I know Lord, it doesn't take You very long to speak when You get ready to speak."

But sometimes God just messes around until the last minute. It seems like it doesn't it, to us? It seems like He's messing around, but He's really not; He is always on time.

"Okay Honey, what is it that you've got to say?" I asked.

She said, "While you were gone the Lord spoke to me and told me, "It's not time to move in, it's time to go. So don't pack to move in the house, pack to move to a trailer house because it's time to go!"

I was so shocked and surprised at what she was saying I could hardly believe it! God had beaten me there and had already told her. That's why He wouldn't tell me anything.

But see, this was a double confirmation.

So if anywhere along the way, the enemy might say, "What are you doing out here?"

We *both* could say, "God sent us."

We packed up and never spent one night in that brand new home, we left it all behind. The fellow I was working with owed me several thousand dollars.

He said, "I'm not going to pay you, that way you will have to stay!"

"Goodbye to you and the money, I'm going," I replied.

That's what God wants from us; obedience. That was in April of 1960. We left everything, and started out by faith and until this day that's what we're still living by. God has never failed. Hallelujah!

Chapter 2

Stepping out in Faith

Heaven's Currency

The reason the Lord is working in our hearts today, is because He wants to raise us to a higher level in believing Him. It is not impossible for God to do great and mighty things. The only thing that hinders Him is our unbelief. But the root of all sin is unbelief.

You might ask, "Brother Samuel, how do you know that?"

That's where it started, in the Garden of Eden. The devil said, *"hath God said?"* (Gen. 3:1). He made Eve doubt what God really said. God told Adam not to eat of the tree of the knowledge of good and evil before Eve was created, so she heard that message through Adam. It's the same today. We, who are ministers of God, called of God; speak the Word. We can either believe it or doubt it. If we believe it, God will honor it, He honors His Word. When we preach God's Word; God is there to back it up. If we preach our theory, that's too bad because He's not going to back up our theories; but if we say what He said then God will stand behind that. So God is raising us just like His disciples when He came here in person. He chose and hand picked His disciples.

One time Jesus said to them, *"I am glad for your sakes that I was not there, that you may believe"* (John 11:15 NKJV).

When Jesus went back into Heaven, He left all of His kingdom and everything that pertains to the kingdom of God in the hands of twelve, three and a half year old Christians. Most of the time we think of three and a half year old Christians as being babies, but He invested everything in them and they would carry on His work in the earth.

Did you know we're living in the finishing of God's plan since the beginning of time? The full gospel church as we know it today, the Holy Ghost filled empowered church; started out by the marvelous power of God working miracles of all kinds; which caused his disciples to be hated, persecuted and commanded not to preach or teach anymore in Jesus' name.

They went back to where they met and had prayer and said, *"God, just stretch forth your hand and do great and mighty things"* (See Acts 4:30).

They were praying for the very thing that was bringing them persecution. Now the reason that they could do all these things was because they received that faith that came from seeing Jesus walking on the water; feeding the 5,000 people with five little loaves and two fish; and seeing Him do many other miracles. The blind eyes would see, the leapers were cleansed, the dead were raised and all these things. He was doing that to increase their faith because they were going to follow in His footsteps; and they were going to keep the ministry that He started here on earth, going until it reached down to us. And we are reaching those that will be reaching others also.

So the Lord wants to make known to us by many infallible proofs that, "I AM the same today as I was yesterday."

We quote that Scripture, *"Jesus Christ, the same yesterday, and today, and forever"* (Heb. 13:8). It is easy to quote sometimes, but it takes the Holy Spirit to put it in our hearts.

Jesus said, *"and does not doubt in his heart, but believes that those things he says will be done, he will have whatever he says"* (Mark 11:23 NKJV).

So the Lord is working on us so He can work through us. The purpose of this book is to make known the wonderful works of God in our day. I don't believe the acts of the apostles are closed out. I believe God is still moving in mighty ways through His Spirit in the earth today. That is a little more difficult for us to believe here in the United States because we have everything just right. We have everything coming so easy, but the Lord in spite of all that wants to make known to us that all this is coming from Him.

You may say, "I'm earning everything I have by working."

But if a stroke or something affected your brain, you couldn't even feed yourself, or tie your shoes. So it's still coming from God, isn't it? He wants us to know that our life is in Him, and in Him nothing is impossible.

The Lord has spoken to me and confirmed it by many witnesses that He wanted the things He has been doing in our life over a period of time to be put in a book, so that people could read it and have their faith increased. So they can know that He is Lord. If you're saved He is your Lord and He's not partial to people. He is partial to faith.

Faith is the currency of Heaven. If you had all the money you wanted you could go buy whatever you wanted. The only thing that keeps you from getting a lot of the things you want is that you don't have the money to do it. But see, that currency doesn't work with God. It doesn't matter how much money you have. It's just as if I brought a whole pocketful of Belize money up here, I couldn't go to the store and buy anything with it; they would not even honor it.

"Take it back to Belize. It'll buy things there, but it won't buy anything here," they would say.

That's the way it is with Heaven. Heaven knows faith currency. It doesn't know U.S. dollars, Belize dollars, or anything else; it knows faith. Faith is the currency of Heaven.

So the Lord wants to increase our faith because He wants to do greater things. Not only just to meet our needs but He wants to do great things through us, to others and for others; so that He might be glorified. To let people know that He's not just a God of Saturday, Sunday, or Monday; He is God all the time and for everyone. That's why we have church. And that's why God put ministers in the body of Christ; to increase our faith, to lift us up, to encourage us. Our Father does really want to bless us because we are His children. How many of you have children that you just enjoy doing things for? Of course we do because they are our children. We are His children and He wants to do great things for us.

Heritage of Faith

As a young man I had very little growing up but I had something that was so valuable. That was to travel with my mom and dad who lived strictly by faith. They left me a heritage of faith. At the age of seventeen I got married, but before that I had our two bedroom home almost completed. I built it myself by the age of seventeen. The Lord began to move in my behalf and restore everything I didn't have earlier in my life.

The Lord said, "I'm going to bless you and give you everything you ever wanted," and He did that.

So before I turned eighteen I had my first house built and was already married. The Lord was blessing me abundantly. As time went on I finally bought out the contractor that I was working with and went into contracting for myself and had my own crew. That was so beautiful because when we would be working and one of the men that worked for me would get sick, we would just go in a back bedroom and have a prayer meeting. We didn't take him to the hospital or call the doctor; we called Jesus, and I'm telling you, it worked.

Restored Arm

I had an ambition to become the best plasterer in the business. That was really the going thing in southern California back in the '50s. I wanted to be the best plasterer in San Bernardino County, and that is a huge county.

They had a project called, "The Homearama Homes," in which many contractors would pick out a piece of land and each would build a house. Then they would have open house and let everyone go through these homes and see who they wanted to build their home for them. So I was chosen to do the Homearama home for this company. It felt good to be chosen because these were special homes. They were going to be really idolized. So to be chosen to do that house was a great honor to me.

We went out there and had just gotten started. We were working in a living room with a vaulted ceiling and over the big bay window was a drop, about ten or twelve inches; fancy is all it was. I got my "hawk" full of "mud" and started down that scaffold to put the "scratch coat" on the ceiling over that little drop over the bay window and my foot slipped. I went straight through that bay window! My trowel in hand broke the window and all my weight came down right on the bend of my arm. It cut all the nerves, all the blood vessels, and everything down to the bone. That looked like the end of my career and possibly my arm! They took me to the hospital; but I almost bled to death before we got there because there was a train on the track and they couldn't get me there really quickly. When I came to there was a cast on my arm that was on there for quite awhile. My dad came out to see me and we were praying.

We were just asking God, "What now?"

Because the doctor told me that I would never do this profession again. It takes tremendous muscle in your arm to put all that "mud" on the ceiling and walls. On a three bedroom house, we would put the first coat on the outside of the house. Then we would do all the inside of the house in eight hours and go home; just two plasterers. When you would drive up early in the morning there would be a huge pile of sand, and by that evening it was all gone. All the cement, plaster, everything that was there, was all on the ceilings and walls in those houses. It had to be half an inch thick on the ceilings and walls, so it took a lot of strength to do that, and I had no strength whatsoever left in my right arm.

One day my dad said, "Let's go see this brother God has been using in the gift of healing. Let's just go see him and have prayer together."

We went to see him, and he didn't make a great big to-do about it. He just simply prayed and asked the Lord to put everything back together. They couldn't feed the blood back into my arm because it was in the bend of my arm and the main artery had been cut, so they had to feed blood into the smaller vessels, and they didn't know if it would work or not. The life is in the blood, so if the blood didn't flow there, my arm would die and they would have to remove it. But he prayed and we believed. God didn't do an instant miracle. It didn't happen instantly but it started getting better quickly. I went back to the doctor and they would give me this little ball to squeeze. When they took the cast off in six weeks, they would put my arm on the table and it would just fall over, there wasn't any strength there. So we just kept believing and thanking God for the healing of my arm.

The Scripture says, "*[The Lord] calls those things which do not exist as though they did*" (Rom. 4:17 NKJV).

Didn't He create us with the same ability to do that? We don't go by what we see; we go by what we believe. When we believe then we see. He said, *"these signs shall follow those who believe"* (Mark 16:17).

He didn't say the believers would follow the signs but the signs would follow the believers. So regardless of how it felt we praised God for healing my arm.

I said, "Lord you gave me this arm and you're going to heal it. In fact, you've already done it, for by your stripes I'm already healed. I just don't see it happening right now, but I believe that it's in Your will that I have my arm. I need this arm."

I went back a few days later to get a test and see how it was coming and the needle moved a little bit when I squeezed on the ball.

The doctor got excited, and said, "There's something happening in there!"

"Yes there is! There's something happening in there, doctor. We've been praying and we are believing that God is healing my arm. Something is happening!" I said.

The next time I went back the needle went a little farther, and it just kept getting better and better. In a very short time I was back on the job plastering again.

Dream Fulfilled

That's what our God can do. He wants to do these things. All He asks us to do is believe. Now don't confess negative things if you're trying to believe with your heart.

We need to confess, "I have faith, and I believe God."

That wasn't the end of the story. They had a man that I had worked with on the job many times who was very fast. Way back in the early '50s, they paid him $5.00 and hour and that was a lot back then, but he was worth it because he really did a fast job and a good job. Now my dream was, to one day, be faster than him; but when I got my arm hurt really badly it looked like that was the end of that dream. But I want to tell you something, when we ask Jesus for His help; He comes on the scene and makes all the difference. So when I went back to my job and had my own crew, I hired that man. Now he was working for me! When they put us in exactly same sized rooms where he did one and I did the other I walked out of the room before he did! I was so happy because the Lord helped me achieve my dream. He loves us. He cares for us. If you have a dream, and it's a legal dream, He will help you get there.

He told Jeremiah, *"I know my plans I have for you, and they are good."* (See, Jer. 29:11 NIV)

Then He comes back in the Holy Spirit to help us get there. We couldn't get there without Him. You know why? We have an adversary that comes to keep us from achieving the goal, but greater is He that lives in us than he that is against us. God is the greater one and He lives in us. By His Spirit He is there. So the Lord let me achieve that.

After my arm healed completely I built my home.

Going into God's Plan

During the time of waiting, for about three and a half years from the time God called us into His ministry, until the time He said it was time to go, I was preparing to take care of myself. I got a gas station and a garage going and leased it to a friend. I was making all kinds of preparations to provide for my own needs.

So that when we got out there on the field people wouldn't have to be burdened saying, "We've got a preacher evangelist coming we need to help them out."

I was trying to do this all on my own. The man that was my contracting partner owed me several thousand dollars.

He said, "I'm keeping your money, I'm not going to pay you because I don't want you to go!"

"Well, you just keep it because I'm going anyway," I replied.

That poor man kept God's money. When they take money from us it's God's money because we belong to Him. So he wound up losing everything and I went on in the ministry.

When we got out there on the field, the first place we went was a place called Deer, Arkansas. It was way back in the Ozarks; very few people know where the place is. We had four children at the time. My dad and mom came up there, and we set up this old tent and began to have tent meetings. People came and God began to work, but there was no money. We were there for six weeks. That's how they used to have revivals, not three days but six weeks! In six weeks all that came in was $27.00. I was used to making over a hundred dollars a day.

Some people say, "If God asks me to go, I'll go."

God wants us to be willing, yet He may never ask you to go; but He is pleased with that commitment. He said, *"If you are willing and obedient, you shall eat the good of the land"* (Isa.1:19 NKJV). We first have to be willing, don't we? Then sometimes He does ask us to give it all away to step out. He doesn't ask everyone to do that but He wants that kind of commitment from everyone of us; because that's the way He can direct our life into His plan, which is far greater than anything we could ever plan for our life.

The gas station didn't work out, that fell through. The man that owed me money didn't repay me, and the gentleman who bought my business wasn't sending me anything either.

So I was out in the woods way back in the hills, crying out to God saying, "I really wanted to provide for myself. God, why was it was all cut off."

This is what the Lord told me, "I wanted you to preach faith. You can't preach it unless you live by it."

We must be first partakers of the fruit. Why did He want me to preach faith? He wanted me to preach faith because He wants to increase our faith.

The Lord is not up there pointing His finger saying, "I wish you would believe."

No, He says, "If you would just believe, I could do this for you."

Search the Scriptures. Take your reference and look at how many times in the Bible it talks about believing. There are a lot of times in there. He just wants us to believe. He's going to do the work. All He's asking us to do is believe. We were there for six weeks and we left that place. There were people saved, healed and filled with the Holy Spirit.

People would come and bring some vegetables out of their garden, crying and say, "I wish we had some money to give you."

I would weep with them because I felt their heart. All the times God blessed me I gave and gave. I enjoy giving, and when you're in a place where you can't really give, it makes you feel bad. I knew they felt bad, so I felt bad for them.

"If you brought me money I'd just have to buy groceries, so thank you for the vegetables," I would tell them.

We left that place and went to another place about thirty miles from there, and used an old school building for two weeks of meetings there. In those two weeks, $270.00 came in. I tell you, God is faithful.

Key of Faith

Right at the close of those meetings we got word that my wife's little brother's horse got scared and kicked him in the face. He lost his sight and hearing and it looked like he wasn't going to live at all. They called and asked us to come. We wouldn't have been able to go if God hadn't have supplied. That second place looked just as poor as the first. It's not so much how it looks, it's how God chooses to do it. Did you know the trying of our faith is more precious than gold?

Sometimes I say, "Lord, the gold sure would look good."

Do we enjoy the trying of our faith? No, we really don't enjoy the trying of our faith, but that's what keeps our faith alive. If you don't ever use your muscles, you will lose them. Faith is something that needs to be exercised constantly.

So we were able to go out to southern California and be with them. When we got there however, they couldn't do anything for him in their hospital. So my father-in-law and I took him in their car and drove him to the hospital in San Diego.

On the way my father-in-law asked me, "What is faith?"

He was an old cowboy and had lived all of his life that way. They are a very hard type to reach because they are tough. If you're really a cowboy you have to be tough. The rest of his family went to the Pentecostal church there in town, and one of the elders was his brother. He had lived a very ungodly life but when this happened he called for the elders to pray for his son. It was the only time he had ever done something like that.

The elders came, and when they got there they said, "You should not have called us because you are not worthy to ask God to heal your son."

He was telling me this as we were driving to San Diego. What bothered him was that they told him he didn't have any faith and should not ask God to heal his son, after the kind of life he had been living. This hit me so hard because here he was about to surrender his heart to the Lord and he had made the first move.

The Bible says, *"Is any sick among you? Let him call for the elders of the church; and let them pray for him, anointing him with oil in the name of the Lord; And the prayer of faith shall save the sick, and the Lord shall raise him up"* (James 5:14-15).

How many of you know that the Lord loves sinners? He came to this world to seek and to save the ones who are lost. He doesn't heal us because we are righteous. He heals us because it is His desire as our Father to see us well. So I tried to break faith down into the simplest form so that he could understand.

"Faith simply believes God meant what He said. Whatever He says that's what He means. If we'll just believe that's what it means, we'll receive it. It's just as simple as that," I said.

Now it put me in a spot because I didn't want to go against the elders of the church, and yet, he was hurting inside. He was hurting because instead of receiving him, and praying with him, and believing with him that God would not only save his son but his soul as well, they turned him out. How many churches have been guilty of doing that? It's so sad.

So I said, "Lord help me, I don't want to go against the elders."

I just began to turn his focus on Jesus instead of on the failure of the elders of the church. We got their boy in the hospital in San Diego, and parked our car way at the back of this huge parking lot. We found this little bed and breakfast near there and rented a room. The second day we were there I went out to the car to be with the Lord for a while because I was really concerned about my young brother-in-law. I asked God what He really wanted to do in this situation. I turned on the radio and was listening to some gospel music and meditating, when my father-in-law walked up to the car and got in. He still wanted to know about this *faith*, so we talked for a little bit and then got out of the car. I shut the door and the door locked. Then I remembered the key was still in the ignition! I didn't want to break any windows to get in, and we needed to go check on their son, so we went back to the hospital and checked. He was about the same, but I couldn't rest. My father-in-law went to get a cup of coffee.

"I'm going to go get the keys out of the car," I told him.

He asked, "How are you going to do that?"

"I don't know, but I'm going to come back with the keys," I replied.

As I walked across the parking lot I saw a piece of wire there that somebody had used who had locked their keys up also.

Something said, "Pick it up."

"No, I'm not going to take this wire because I know this car, and using this wire won't work," I said to myself.

It was an Oldsmobile and when the little side windows are rolled up you are not going to get in that car that way. Of course we didn't have AAA or any of those things in those days.

So while I was walking across the parking lot I said, "Lord, you are the only one who knows how I can get into this car."

I'm telling you, we aren't talking about religion, or doctrines, we're talking about a life of just walking with the Lord.

The Bible says of the Lord, "*In all your ways acknowledge Him, and He shall direct your paths*" (Prov. 3:6 NKJV). If we will acknowledge Him that's our part, then He directs our paths. So I didn't know what to do, but my eyes were upon Him.

After I asked the Lord how to get into the car, He spoke to me and said, "There will be a man that will come and park on the other side of you, take his key and unlock the door."

He spoke just as plain as day!

"Thank you Lord," I said.

We were on the back side of this large parking lot, not many cars are coming and going there; so I stood by the car and in a little while a car drove up.

The man got out of the car and started walking by me and I said to him, "Excuse me, sir. I locked the keys inside my car and was wondering if I could use your key to open my door?"

He looked at me like I was crazy because we didn't even have the same type of car. So he goes over there full of unbelief; stuck the key in, turned it, and it didn't do anything.

I said, "Thank you, sir," and he left.

Then Lord said, "He didn't believe."

So I said, okay, there must be somebody else coming then. In a little while another car came and parked on the other side of him.

He walked by me just the same way, and I said, "Excuse me, sir. I locked the keys inside my car and was wondering if I could use your key to open my door?"

He looked at me with the same unbelief. So while we are walking, I just reached over and took the key right out of his hand; put the key in the door, unlocked the door and handed him his key back. I'm telling you; the guy almost fell over! So I got the key out of my car and I went back praising the Lord.

My father-in-law inquired, "Did you get the keys?"

"Yeah, here they are," I said.

He asked me how I got them and I said, "The same way you've been asking me about faith; and I told you to simply believe what God said and He'll bring it to pass. The Lord told me that there would be a man who would park next to me. He told me to get his car key and unlock my door, and that's exactly how I got in the car."

You know, that got to him. It just healed all that hurt and all those things that were bothering him. The miracle of God healed his heart.

I'm telling you, God is real. And you know, until many years after that; every time I'd see him he'd remind me of how I got the keys out of that car. Now see, that wasn't me; I only obeyed. That was Jesus that did that. That second guy didn't have any faith either and I could see it. So I didn't trust him. I just took the key right out of his hand and unlocked the door. It wasn't even the same kind of car, the same year or anything. How many times have you tried somebody else's key to get into your car? You can use a bunch of them, but they won't open the door. But you know what? We are in the flesh but we're filled with the Spirit. Now the flesh sometimes likes to take the preeminence. We like to do it our way, right? That is the battle I have. I know this temple is God's temple but Sam lives here too; and that is the battle we all have. There is a battle between the flesh and the Spirit. The Spirit believes God, the Spirit is God. The flesh is the one that doubts. So if we learn to walk in God's Spirit, in His presence then His work will follow. I believe that the Lord worked this to heal a broken sinner's heart. He did it by simply doing what He said.

Our Eyes Are on Him

We went back to Arkansas after this was over and began to minister in tent meetings in many different places. The Lord sent us to a little town of Dover. We set up the tent there, and I'm telling you, rain storms came that looked like they'd blow the tent away. Through lightning and thunder we were out there trying to hold it to keep it from blowing away. We had a lot of adversity.

Not really anything great happened except two young men gave their hearts to the Lord. Now I've heard of "holy rollers" ever since I was born, but I never had seen one until then. My sister was playing the accordion by the side of the tent and one of these young men made contact, got his sins forgiven, and he was so happy he hit the sawdust rolling. He rolled right out from under the tent. In the meantime, he hit the chair where my sister was sitting. She went one way, and the chair went the other. So she got up, dusted the sawdust off of her, picked up her accordion; sat back down, and was playing, when he came back under the tent. He hit her and knocked her back down again.

I said, "That's a genuine "holy roller."

Just a few weeks after we closed the meeting that young man was driving down the mountain, lost control of his vehicle and was killed. The Lord loves us. I believe He sent us there just for those two young men. Other people came and were blessed, but those were the only two that accepted the Lord in that meeting. It's worth it all. One soul won to God is worth more than the whole world. *"the world is passing away, and the lust of it; but he who does the will of God abides forever"* (1 John 2:17 NKJV). Every soul that comes into the world is eternal. God wants every eternal soul to be with Him through all of eternity. That's why He sent His Son. He didn't send Him down here for a vacation. He didn't send Him down here to start a new movement, or a new organization; He sent Him here to redeem us; all those that had come before Him and those that would come after Him. He came to redeem us and to restore us back into that place of fellowship and relationship with the Father that He knew with Adam and Eve before the fall in the garden. That's exactly why He came. He came because the Father wanted us back. He wanted that relationship back with men; His masterpiece of a creation. He longs for us; He desires us so much that He gave His only Son to redeem us. He still loves us that much today.

We were ministering in different places in Arkansas and working with this church. I believe ministry needs a home church just like we all need a home church. We all need each other. We're not complete in ourselves, we are complete in Him, and in Him is the body of Christ. We would take some young men with us that felt they were called into the ministry, and give them a chance to share and preach, and let them obey the Lord. We were way back up in the mountains and had church every night. Saturday was usually the biggest night. This particular Saturday, the church was packed out but the spirits of the people were really down.

We would ask people if they had something to say and they'd just say, "No, I don't have anything to say."

We'd ask the next one and they would say, "No."

We would ask if anyone had a testimony and they'd say, "No;" just nothing.

So I preached that night with almost no anointing.

Now there are different kinds of anointing. There is a true and a false anointing. Sometimes there is no anointing at all. Did you know there is a self-anointing? A self-anointing is when we get all hyped up on ourselves. There is also the true anointing and an anointing that; when people are hungry, it just pulls it out of you. Then there is a prophetic anointing that comes on you and whether people are listening or not, it just pours out of you. It's a prophetic anointing that is coming directly from the throne. There weren't any of those that night. So since we have to be in season and out of season; I just opened the Bible, read some Scriptures, and asked if anyone needed prayer, but I got nothing. So we closed the meeting that night and went home.

I saw these young men that we took with us looking so discouraged and disappointed.

"Look, don't let what you experienced tonight discourage you, we're in the process of learning. It's not by our might and it's not by our power but it's; *"by My Spirit, says the Lord of hosts"* (Zec. 4:6 NKJV). I will guarantee you that the Lord was in that service tonight; but He doesn't always move the same way. So I want to encourage you because we can't encourage the people if we are discouraged," I told them.

We were back on Sunday morning, and it felt like all heaven came down. I'm telling you, we don't look at the circumstances, we look at Him. We need to always keep our eyes on Him.

Prayed into Arizona

When I was just a little boy, my Dad, my Grandfather, and another minister went to Globe from Phoenix, Arizona to have a tent revival. Many people were saved, but they had nowhere to go to church. So they bought a piece of property and put up a little building and that became their church. It was called Globe Canyon Church and it remains there today. Many years after it was built, a minister friend and his wife served as Pastors there for many years. They also ministered out on the Apache reservation near there. After they retired they moved back to Arkansas, near Hot Springs. We fellowshipped often with them.

One day he asked me if I'd take him back out to Globe, Arizona to visit the church and to take some food and clothing to the reservation. Even though he was much older than me, I struggled to keep up with him. We ministered on the reservation and gave out the food and clothing and had a few nights services in that little church building.

A couple of ladies that I called "mothers in Israel" had been faithful to that little church for many years, and they knew how to pray. They also got the ladies at the reservation praying too. They began to pray, "God send Brother Samuel to Pastor this church."

They even went out to the reservation where we were ministering and asked me if I would be their Pastor.

I told them, "It would take God telling me because I have no desire to go to the deserts of Arizona."

I like the trees. That's why I like East Texas.

When we left, they said, "We'll give you until Christmas to be here."

We were there by Thanksgiving! Do you know what happened to me?

When I got back to Arkansas and sang that song that says, "I'll go where You want me to go, Dear Lord...," the Lord said to me, "Go back to Arizona."

So we loaded up and went back. We got there with less than five dollars, and the church had less than five dollars in the church treasury. It was in a sad, run-down condition, inside and out.

I said, "Well here we are, Lord. What do You want me to do? I have a family, and You know it takes money to live. What do You want me to do? Do You want me to get a job?"

The Lord told me, "No."

He told me that he had sent me to build the spiritual house and repair the natural house. So we began to do that. Meanwhile, the Lord began to work and move, but not as fast as I wanted Him to. I wanted to get this thing done right away.

No Dentist Needed

When I was preaching out at the reservation I met a Pastor over the mountain in Superior, Arizona, and we kept in touch.

He called me one day and said, "Brother Samuel, we had an evangelist here and something happened at home and he had to leave. Tonight is the last night of the revival. Could you please come over and preach for us tonight?"

I told him I would have to call him back. I found somebody that would take charge of the service at our church that night because I really felt like I needed to go. So we went over and I preached for them. Now it's hard to follow in somebody else's shoes. This evangelist had been preaching during the entire revival and then I stepped in. But I don't try to do my own thing; I try to let God lead me. Only God knows what the people need. I just prayed that God would speak through me and that I would share what they needed. I prayed for the words for the people at the right time and at the right place. So the Lord moved mightily in that service that night. At the end I invited anyone who needed anything from the Lord to come forward. People came forward and we prayed for them.

This one lady came up and I asked her what she needed. She had a list of things wrong with her.

"You just really need a general overhaul then," I said.

I called on Jesus, the mechanic. I knew He had all the parts she needed. If you have a Cadillac, they have parts for them. If you have an Oldsmobile, they have parts for them. No matter what car you have, there are parts to fix them if they break. Well God has parts to fix everything that is wrong with us as well. If He can take a rib out of a man and make a woman from it, He can do anything. He is the great physician. So we just prayed and asked God to heal her from the top of her head to the soles of her feet. She went home that night and was she in for a surprise. When she went in the bathroom to brush her teeth, she could see that every tooth had been filled! She had a lot of bad teeth but she didn't have the money to go get them fixed. God filled every tooth in her mouth! Before this happened the pastor didn't believe in that.

Her husband wasn't a believer.

When she looked in the bathroom mirror and saw her teeth, she called, "Honey, come in here quick!"

He thought something bad was wrong with her. She opened her mouth wide and every tooth in her mouth was filled!

The Pastor learned about this the next morning, called me and said, "Brother Sam, you won't believe this because I didn't believe it either. I have heard about people getting their teeth filled and I didn't believe in that; but God did it anyway. We asked Him to heal her from the top of her head to the soles of her feet, and God did it!"

It certainly made a believer out of the pastor, that ladies' husband, and a whole bunch of other people.

I've seen services where God was filling people's teeth and everybody went around with their mouth open; and you could just see those teeth growing in their mouths. Is that impossible with God? Absolute not! What is it that God can't do? When it comes to what we have need of, there is no limitation.

So the Lord established us there in Arizona. For many days I would be up in the Pinal Mountains near the church, crying out, "God, teach me your ways. Give me understanding because I want the truth. Only the truth can set the captives free. Only the truth will stand forever. All the philosophies will fall by the wayside. All the doctrines of men don't have any preeminence. God, give me the truth."

He revealed many things to me.

Giving God His Work

There was a time when the church wasn't growing the way I wanted it to. One day when I had been there for many days, I asked God what else I could do.

The Lord spoke to me and said, "You have carried it long enough, why don't you let Me have it?"

I had been carrying it. I had been feeling like it was my responsibility, but if I am obeying Him, then it's His responsibility. However, as long as I tried to carry it He would let me carry it.

It was then that I threw up both hands and said, "Jesus, it's yours!"

From that day on, God began to move in such tremendous ways. People began selling their houses in other towns and moving to where we were just to be a part of what God was doing. Every morning we had prayer meetings and Bible studies at the church and God was moving in mighty ways. People were afraid to stay at home because they knew they would miss what God was going to do. You never knew what God was going to do because no two services were the same.

The Holy Spirit Speaks

There are many things I could say about that, but there is just one I want to say. Our daughter loved the Apache Indians. We had a few families that came to our church who were Apache. I taught my people that when you walk through the doors the service starts. We come here to worship God. When you came in the door people would come and begin praying at the altar. There we saw God filling people with the Holy Ghost, saving souls, and doing all kinds of things before the service ever started. That was God moving, and that's what happened on this particular night.

People came and began to gather around the altar and all of a sudden some of the Apache Indians came over to me, and said, "Brother Sam, come here, we want you to hear what is going on!"

The Lord had filled our daughter with the Holy Ghost and she was speaking in fluent Apache! They understood every word she was saying.

"I Want to Go to Belize"

We had built a living room onto the small parsonage, repaired the building and made improvements there. Quite often after the service dismissed I would stay in the church and talk to the Lord. I would just pray and enjoy His presence. He enjoys fellowshipping with me, and I enjoy fellowshipping with Him.

Right in the middle of all this sweet fellowship time, Jesus said to me, "I want to go to Belize, will you go with me?"

I did not want to go there. God was moving in mighty ways right where I was. I didn't know anyone in Belize. I wasn't looking for adventure. I was happy. But God gave me time to make my decision.

After awhile I told Him, "If you're going to Belize, I don't want to stay here by myself."

I had read in the Scripture when the cloud moved, the people moved. If people didn't move when the cloud moved, they got left behind. I didn't want to be left behind. I had already found out that God's provision was in the place where He wanted me. So I told the church that the Lord had asked me to do a hard thing. He had asked me to take Him to this country. When I told them that, they told me that they would give me a two year leave of absence. At the time we had young children who were in school.

I had heard sermons where thousands of people had been saved in one night. I assumed since Belize was such a small country, I ought to be able to get them all converted in a short time. So I agreed with them and took a two year leave of absence. One of the men in the church took over for me. I found out that when you go where there is nothing but total darkness, it doesn't all happen overnight. Also when people come to Christ they need discipleship. So when two years was over I came back to resign. I told them that the Lord was not through with me in Belize yet. There had been people coming to Christ, but now they needed help; understanding and teaching. So they told me that they would extend it another two years.

Another Offer

We wound up being in Belize for twenty-nine years. I was offered many different positions. One offer was to travel with mission groups around the world who were just teaching Pastors. When the Lord told me that He was going to bless me and give me everything I ever wanted, He also told me that if I would be faithful to Him, He would send me around the world. I didn't want to hear that part, because at that time I still told myself I was not going to be a preacher and I knew God wouldn't be sending me on vacation all around the world. If He was sending me that meant that I was going to be preaching.

I was in Belize when this mission group called and asked me to join their team. I thought this might be what God had told me through that prophecy, so I went to Southern California to meet with them and see what they had to tell me. These men met together with me and told me what was on their hearts. They told me I was wasting my time being in Belize, and they wanted me to be a part of their team instead. They wanted me to go to different countries with them and they already had it set up. They would go to different parts of the world and meet with Pastors of churches and share with them. Then they would go back and take it to their congregations. They said it was more effective that way.

I thanked them for their confidence, but I told them there was one thing I needed and that was confirmation by God. So I told them to go back to their homes that night and pray and see what God says, and I will go back to my hotel room and pray, even if it takes all night. I thought that maybe this was the "around the world" thing that God had prophesied to me years ago. If this is what God wanted from me, then I would go; but it wasn't exciting to me. I don't like to travel. So we all went and prayed. I told God that if this was an open door and this is what He wanted me to do, then I am ready to do it.

When daylight came the answer came to me just as clearly as anything.

God said to me, "I am not through with you in Belize."

So we came back and met the next morning and I asked them if the Lord had told them anything the previous night.

They said, "No, He didn't say anything, but we still feel the same way."

I told them that God did speak to me. I told them what He said, and they thought I was being rebellious. They quoted different Scriptures to me. I told them I appreciated their confidence and offer and that I would be praying for them. What they did was good. Teaching Pastors to be leaders and to go back and share the truth with their churches is a good thing, but that was not what God had for me. I believe that if God gives you a duty to do, you need to keep on doing it until He tells you to do something else. We, as God's children, should feel that responsibility. We are all a part of the body of Christ, but the Lord wants us to be faithful.

The Bible says, *"for many are called, but few chosen"* (Matt.

20:16). God does the calling and the choosing. It is our job to be faithful. So they wrote me off their list. They told me again that I was wasting my time. But I told them that my time did not belong to me, my time belonged to God.

After that I went back, and since then, God has done marvelous things in Belize. We had to press through all kinds of witchcraft, darkness; and even people that said they were Christians, but didn't know anything about the Lord. The Bible talks about people who have a "form of godliness" but don't know about the power. I believe the Gospel has power. It did back in the early days, and it still does today. In fact, we are a part of that same church that started on that "Day of Pentecost."

So we began going up and down the country. We met a missionary there that had been there for several years and had established a few churches up and down the Western districts. He took us in and we lived in a little hut thing made out of canvas. When it rained we got wet. So finally one day, he told us that he would let us move into one of the rooms in his uncompleted home for the elderly.

You know, things don't always look really exciting when you're obeying God, but just keep on keeping on. One attribute of faith is, going on regardless of how you feel. Just keep on going. If the Lord is with you, He will make the way. We began to have weekly revivals in the next village over in a little church. Every day we would work on the old folks' home trying to get it ready, because at the time, when people got old they had nothing. Social Security didn't exist in Belize back then, and the government did not provide places for them to live. We continued to work and finally got the home completed. Then the well went bad in the village, and we repaired that. The other missionary's car broke down and we fixed that too. This little senior lady we knew had a modern washing machine that broke; and we fixed that. We just spent our time serving Jesus and doing what we could. The Bible says that Jesus went about doing good and healing all that were oppressed of the devil. I knew that I may not be able to go around healing all that were oppressed of the devil, but I could go around doing good. We can all do that. The things that the Lord would have you do, just do it with all your heart.

Mayan Ruins

One day some people took us across the Guatemalan border over to the Mayan Ruins of Tikal because they wanted to give us a little break. It is quite a large portion of ruins and in the years that had gone by thousands of people lived in that area. They still don't know what happened to the people. The ruins are still there but the people are gone. While we were there we saw a huge temple. The steps to the temple were very narrow and almost straight up. There was also a big courtyard where there were stones that served as places to offer human sacrifices. Across the courtyard there was another big temple. The amazing thing was that you didn't have to have a P.A. system. You could stand at one temple and talk to somebody across the courtyard at the other temple. I don't know how the Mayans did all that construction, but that is exactly the way it was. While I was up there I sat down and began looking out on the vast area below. From the top you could see the villages and areas where people had lived and offered their sacrifices.

It was then that I began to weep.

I inquired, "God, what happened to all these people? They never had a chance to hear the Gospel. They had no opportunity."

Have you ever wondered about that? I was sincerely asking God what had happened to these thousands of people that never had a chance to hear the Gospel. But guess what? He didn't answer me.

In other words, it was none of my business; but what He did say was this; "You can't do anything about those that have already gone; but you can do something about the ones that are still here."

There are many questions we have that we don't need the answers to. What we need to know is what we can do now for those who are still here. God had laid different areas of Belize in front of me where people were just living the way they had lived for hundreds of years. It seemed as if their own government and the rest of the world had forgotten about them; and worst of all, they had never heard the name of Jesus. They had never seen a Bible. That day God did something in me. When God lays the burden of souls on your heart you will find a way; and if you don't, I guarantee you will pray for somebody else to. You will pray for salvation for lost souls because you realize that every soul is precious to God.

Hungry for the Word

One day this other brother and I were going through the jungles, and we saw a guy run out in front of us. He just ran out in front of my truck with a machete in his hand, and started waving at me to stop. It was an Indian man, you don't know whether to stop or not, but when you have Jesus, He says I can take care of you, no matter what. Now they live and die by these machetes and they know how to use them, let me tell you.

Anyway, I stopped and rolled down the window to see what he wanted. The man was out of breath and couldn't say anything for awhile. He heard the gospel music playing for miles. He was back in the bush chopping out a little plantation. When they plant, they stick a hole in the ground with a stick and put their seed in it. That's the way they grow their crops.

I had to wait for quite awhile for him to get his breath before he could even say what he wanted. When he finally could catch his breath and say anything, he said, "I heard your music and started running through the jungles just praying, 'God help me to reach the road before he passes on.'"

Do you know what he wanted? A Bible; that is what he ran all those miles for. In the back of that truck I had some Bibles. He was so hungry. He had come from one of the villages where the Lord had moved. He had accepted the Lord, but didn't have a Bible. He just wanted a Bible. Isn't that something? Praise God!

Do you know where that Bible came from? It was one of the old Gideon Bibles that had served its purpose in a motel or hotel somewhere. When they went around and picked up the old ones and gave out the new ones, I got the old ones and took them to Belize and put them back to work. Hallelujah!

Chapter 3

Grace in Action

Looking for a Messiah

I don't know what all the Lord has in mind to do, but I know that He's going to do some great things for us in these days. He has in mind of doing some tremendous things. So don't despise the day of small things because God is a big God and He can do great things.

When God took Abraham's seed into Egypt, He took them there to use Egypt as an incubator to grow a nation. He had promised all the land of Canaan to Abraham's seed but there weren't enough of them to possess the land. So He took them to Egypt and that became the incubator to rise up a strong nation. The Pharaoh saw that they were gaining momentum in a hurry. They were populating fast because God was blessing them. Then the enemy set out to destroy them and to stop them from multiplying.

God blessed them, but hard times came because they would have become totally satisfied to stay in Egypt. So the Lord caused a Pharaoh to be born that forgot all about Joseph and about Abraham's seed. He began to really make it tough on them. He made slaves out of them and they began to desire to get out. Do you have a desire to get out of this old wicked situation that the world is in today?

They began to desire to get out, but they needed a savior. They needed a deliverer. They couldn't get out by themselves. So their whole hope, aim, and desire was for that deliverer. That's what they were looking forward to. They kept looking for this deliverer, this Messiah, this savior to come and take them out of this land of Egypt into the "Promised Land" that God had provided for them.

Many lived and died and never saw it but finally the day came. God took a little humble shepherd and took his shoes off his feet. What made that ground holy? It was the presence of God. It is His presence in us that makes us holy too. Did you know that? What makes a church holy so that when you come in you feel the Lord? It's His presence. God sent Moses down there in answer to their cry because God told Moses that He saw their tears. He knew about the sorrows of His people and heard their cries. That's what He said. Does he see ours today? When we cry and seek God for the lost for those who don't know God, for the wickedness of our generation; He sees and hears. He said, *"I have seen their tears and I have heard their cry. Now I am going to send you down there to bring them out"* (See, Ex.3:7-10). And God was faithful to do that.

Satan is always our adversary. He is the adversary to God and if you're on God's side he is your adversary. Some people don't want Jesus to come because they're about to retire and they want to enjoy their retirement. If you wonder why the trials and the tests are getting harder just remember that this world is not our home we're just passing through. So don't get too settled down here.

Wanting Freedom

For generations Israel was blessed. As long as they kept God as their God they were blessed and no nation could come against them. But when they would forget the Lord and start worshiping idols, then God would let them be overrun. Finally in the days when Jesus came God's people were in bondage to Rome. So they began looking for the Messiah to come and deliver them out of that bondage. They weren't looking to go to Heaven. They were looking to get out of the bondage of the Roman Empire so that they could be free again. We know that this was so because even His own disciples said, *"Grant us that we may sit, one on Your right hand and the other on Your left, in Your glory"* (Mark 10:37 NKJV). One of the last things they said to Him was, *"Lord, will You at this time restore the kingdom to Israel?"* (Acts 1:6 NKJV). What they were looking for was a Messiah to restore back to them the place and the authority they had, and the place with God they had before they sinned against God. Did you know that day came? The day came when that Messiah came.

Hundreds of people had lived and died. Generations had passed and they all looked for the Messiah. The day came when the shepherds were out there in the field just like every other day. They were there taking care of their flocks when all of a sudden they had a visitation of angels. Angels came from Heaven and announced the birth of the "Son of God" in Bethlehem. They were so excited. Can you imagine the excitement in their hearts? Now they would be free from Rome. They said one to another, *"Let us now go to Bethlehem and see this thing that has come to pass, which the Lord has made known to us"* (Luke 2:15 NKJV).

So they took off and found that it was true, the Messiah had come. But He didn't fulfill what they wanted, to be restored back to a free nation. They didn't understand that Jesus was born to die.

He was born to take our place, our sins, our guilt, to take our infirmities and our confusion, to take everything that is absent from the presence of God. He was born to restore everything that man had lost in the Garden of Eden. Through His death there would be that restoration. They did not understand that. So they couldn't receive Him as the Messiah that He really was. This explains why they saw Jesus crucified and give up the ghost. They saw the heavens turn black and the rocks rent and the veil in the Temple was torn. They saw a drastic change take place, but they did not see freedom from the Roman Empire.

God's Plan for Us

Two of his disciples were walking from Jerusalem to Emmaus, and they were so sad because all of their hopes were gone. All of the things that they thought would happen when the Messiah came didn't happen. They were so dejected, so discouraged and so despondent.

We know different facets of that; Peter said, "I'm going to go back to fishing."

All their hopes were gone because it didn't work the way they wanted it to. God had a bigger plan in mind. They didn't have the big picture; they didn't understand the plan of God. They didn't see that we had to come into this thing before they could get what they wanted. God gave us something better.

He said, *"All these died in faith, not having received the promises, that they without us should not be made perfect"* (Heb.11:13 & 40). The "Church" wasn't complete, the "Bride" wasn't complete, and He couldn't do what they thought He came to do, but He is coming again. Now we're living in a generation that's looking for Jesus to come back. That same Jesus that they saw go away will come in like manner as He went away, in a cloud of witnesses. He's coming back in a cloud of witnesses.

Now what are we looking for? What are we wanting now, just to go to heaven and walk on streets of gold? There won't be any more light bills to pay, no more debts, no more sickness, no more pain. That's all there, but what we really long for is to see Jesus, to see the One that made it all possible. To see the One that created heaven and Earth. The One that came and bore our sins, sicknesses and our penalties, and took it all so that we could have life; eternal life, that's what we're looking for. Not just another few days of blessing, but eternal life with Jesus Christ! That's what Christ's coming means to us today.

I think sometimes that this is why the trials and tests and the things of this world are not satisfying and times are getting hard, because otherwise we'd be just as happy to stay here. Just let it go on like it is, just keep it on going, oh Hallelujah; we're having a good life, let's just go on.

But the Lord is saying, "I have something better for you, I have eternal life."

He said, *"In Your [My] presence is fullness of joy"* (Ps. 16:11).

So, I'm looking forward to what God has in mind.

I used to, when I was a young fellow, really enjoyed just sitting and listening to missionaries tell the stories of what God had done on the mission field. I never thought I'd ever be one. I never thought I would be giving testimonies, but I enjoyed that. This is what the Lord wants for each one of us; He wants our basket to be full and our excitement to be full.

He wants us to know, "I'm not just the God of Moses, I'm not just the God of Jacob, but I am your God."

When we know that, we can say, "My Father."

If He is my Father then I'm His son, and you are His son or daughter. We are royalty; we have a royal family that we're connected with!

We didn't deserve it, but He made us worthy because He took our penalty and paid for it, so that we could have His righteousness and eternal life.

In Romans 8:28, Paul said, *"And we know that all things work together for good to those that love God, to those who are called according to His purpose."* Now Paul was very hated, persecuted, beaten; shipwrecked; stoned and left for dead. Yet he said, *"--the things which happened to me have actually turned out for the furtherance of the Gospel"* (Phil. 1:12 NKJV).

It didn't happen to him so he would be defeated, and people would say, "If he was a man of God nothing like this would have happened to him."

He didn't say that, he said, "It's for the furtherance of the Gospel."

He didn't quit going just because he was hated and persecuted.

He said, *"But none of these things move me; nor do I count my life dear to myself, so that I may finish my race with joy, and the ministry which I received from the Lord Jesus, to testify to the Gospel of the grace of God"* (Acts 20:24 NKJV).

So the purpose in sharing these things that the Lord has done is that we might realize that their God is our God, their Father is our Father.

Jesus said at the resurrection, *"I am ascending to My Father and your Father, and to My God and your God"* (John 20:17 NKJV).

If you really comprehend the things I'm sharing, you will get excited. You may not feel like jumping up and down or running around the room, but there's an inward excitement that the devil can't put out!

Asking No Questions

We had a truck load of Bibles that we were taking to new converts in Belize that had never seen a Bible. Aren't we blessed? They had never seen a Bible and never heard the name, "Jesus." We had to carry them in the truck and go as far as it could go and then take a little dory. That's a little boat that's hewn out by hand out of a log, round on the bottom, and very easily tipped over; and if you're not very careful, it will dump you out in the river; it does happen. But we had to get God's Word to people who were born of the Spirit, people who had received Christ. We had some of the Word in us and we shared that Word with them and that Word brought life to them. Then they need that Word. This is our life; *"Man shall not live by bread alone, but by every Word that proceedeth out of the mouth of God"* (Matt. 4:4). This is God's Word, and getting the Word to these people was not an easy task. But we had the great joy of taking the Word to them and seeing the Word of God operate in them.

When people would receive Christ their life was changed. Now, they had nothing of this world's goods. A dirt floor with one room with all the children, sometimes grandchildren; the chickens, dogs and pigs. Everything in that one room. The animals had access because there wasn't anything to keep them out. They had no furniture. If you sat down on anything it was a block of wood. No spoon, fork and knife to eat with, and no napkins. Their roofs were thatched and full of scorpions because the scorpions love those thatched roofs. They are fairly cooler in the summer time because they are pretty thick and it keeps the sun from getting too hot inside. Their stove is an open fire with a little piece of tin over it to cook on. When you would go into the village you might think every house in the village is on fire because all the smoke is coming out through the thatch on the roof. But they can make some of the best tortillas you ever ate because they grind it on a rock with their corn; scald it, grind it out on the rock; pat it out with their hand, and put it there on that tin over the fire to cook. Then when it comes off all hot they put it in a calabash. That's what we would call a gourd, but they call it a calabash. They cut the top out, and put their tortillas in there and it keeps them hot. Then they will serve you iguana caldo (stew), monkey caldo, or stew made out of different kinds of animals.

People have asked me, "What does it taste like?"

"Thank God for spices," I'd say.

You put enough spices on it, you don't know what that is you're eating, and that's a blessing.

The Bible says, *"whatever is set before you, eat, asking no questions, for conscience's sake"* (1 Cor. 10:27).

I've done that a lot of times for my own conscience's sake. I didn't really know or want to know what I was eating. God gives us grace at times like that because we're not used to those kinds of things. That's what they have been raised on, that's what they eat; and so we have to eat it too. If you are there for several days, and you don't eat with them, they don't accept what you've got to say, either. So eat whatever is set before you, asking no questions.

Word of Life

We would watch as God would honor His Word and begin to work in their lives individually, touch their heart and touch their spirit. Jesus made Himself alive in them. We were giving them His Word and He was giving them His life.

Jesus said, *"The Words that I speak unto you, they are spirit, and they are life."* (John 6:63).

They are life; not just something to memorize or to talk about, they bring life. We watched life begin to come into them, and then watch as God would place His hand on people; different ones in the village for leadership. We're talking about miracles. You're not going to change people that have been in their theories, superstitions, and witchcraft. You're not going to change them on your own. I don't care how good a talker you are, you cannot change people. It takes God to change the hearts of people.

Jesus said, *"greater works than these he will do, because I go to My Father"* (John 14:12 NKJV). What is the greatest work to God? The greatest work to Him is greater than walking on water and even greater than raising the dead. It's the transformation of a life that is steeped in sin. He comes by His Spirit and transforms, and that's the greatest miracle of all. And God has given us that honor, to lead people to Christ. The reason Jesus couldn't do that is because He hadn't yet died and rose again. The Gospel had not been completed yet. The Gospel is the death, burial and resurrection of Jesus Christ. That is the Gospel, and it couldn't be preached until He had died and rose again. The world never saw Him again but His disciples did. They were His witnesses that He arose from the dead. Then God confirmed His Word with signs following to prove that He was alive.

So we watched God work in these different places and then we would have like a camp meeting when we would have several days and nights of meetings. We would try to help get the people that we could reach with this little 48 passenger bus. We would have 90 people on that bus making two or three loads a night to get people to these meetings. Ninety people on a 48 passenger bus!

We had a young man that came to help us in the meetings and he just begged me, "Let me drive the bus, Brother Hooper."

I said, "Oh I'd be so glad to, but you wouldn't make the first load till we'd have a broken spring, because the roads are so rough, with 90 people on it; you've got to know how to ease in and ease out and ease over; with that many people to keep from breaking a spring."

So the meetings went on and we were believing God for an out-pouring of the Holy Ghost, just believing God; because we knew that was what was going to set the people "on fire" in Belize. The Holy Ghost being poured out is the fire of God.

John the Baptist said, *"He shall baptize you with the Holy Ghost and with fire"* (Luke 3:16).

We had gone for a few nights just letting God move pouring out His Spirit, preaching the Word. One night as we were ministering and closing, the presence of God filled that tent. There was nobody to catch them, no carpeted floor, nothing but dirt; but they began to be "slain in the Spirit" all over that place, and they would come up speaking in tongues! God began to pour out of His Spirit. It wasn't hype, it wasn't a special thing that we were doing; it was God. God visited that place. In three nights there were over 60 people filled with the Holy Spirit! Now most of these people were the Maya and the Kekchi Indians; who are usually very quiet people. The ladies hardly ever say anything. But you should have seen them when the Holy Ghost filled them; they became like wild Indians--jumping, shouting, praising God and speaking in other languages!

Thirst Quenched

Just across the road from where we had set up this old tent was the Methodist church. It was kind of unusual to see any churches anywhere around there, but there was the Methodist church. Do you know what? They began to fight us.

"That's a bunch of bologna, just a bunch of noise and carrying on," They said.

So the Superintendent of that denomination came down. We were way down in the southern part of Belize, and she came down there to find out what was really going on. Sunday night was the last night of the meeting, and she came. Guess what happened?

"God is in this place," she said, "I want what God is doing here."

She came to me just before the service was dismissed and implored, "Brother Hooper; would you go one more night? I believe if you would just go one more night I 'd get filled with the Holy Ghost."

"We will," I replied.

The Sunday evening service of that meeting lasted seven hours without a break. I'm telling you, when God is there time flies, you forget all about time. Nobody had that hustle and bustle; we have got to get here or we've got to do that. Nobody even wanted to go home. Seven hours Sunday afternoon and night!

So we announced a Monday night meeting, "Okay, we are going on, we'll have a meeting Monday night."

Monday night we had just as many people as Sunday night.

Even though some of her people were against it, it didn't matter to her, because she was hungry for God. It doesn't matter what is written over the door or where you've been, or what you know; when you're hungry for God He will meet you. He will do something for you.

"Blessed are they who do hunger and thirst after righteousness; for they shall be filled" (Matt. 5:6).

I'll never forget that Monday night service. This lady was sitting right up close to the front and on the edge of her seat. She could hardly wait for the altar call. When that altar call time came she hit that altar and it wasn't but a few minutes until she was speaking a heavenly language! Now I'm telling you, God set her on fire and it turned the Methodists on. God is no respecter of persons, it doesn't matter; He loves everybody. Praise God!

Catch for the Kingdom

During that meeting a lot of people came and gave their hearts to the Lord. In that area we had some East Indians, some native Belizean, the Maya and the Kekchi Indians. Quite a few different nationalities were there.

This lady came and gave her heart to the Lord, and said, "I wish you would talk to my husband, he is so hard. Would you please come to our little store front place of business in the town of Punta Gorda; and talk to my husband?"

"Sure, sure I will," I said.

So the next day I went there. Now everybody of course in that whole part of the country knew me, so I didn't have to introduce myself. He saw me coming and he was already prepared for me. He was a back slidden Jehovah's Witness and he was very hard and bitter. All kinds of corruption was on the inside of him, and when he saw me coming, he took it out on me. He poured it out and it was regurgitating all over me.

The Lord spoke to me in my spirit and said, "Just hold your peace, be still, don't say anything."

So he just poured it out, poured it out, and poured it out; until finally it was getting later in the evening, and I said, "Well, pardon me, but I need to go and get ready for church tonight. I'll be praying for you."

He didn't know what to say, and that was the only thing I had said.

Then I said, "I'll see you tomorrow."

I wanted to let him know that I was coming back so that he could get all the rest of it ready. Anything he had forgotten or left out he could have it ready, because I know one thing; my God is bigger than the roaring of the lion, the roaring of the enemy seeking whom he may devour. He roars, but that's all he can do because Jesus took his teeth out.

So the next day I went back. He saw me coming and he wasn't through yet, he just poured it on. God's Holy Spirit inside kept me calm. It's not natural to have people chew you out and tell all kinds of terrible things about God, preachers and Christians; just regurgitating everything bad that they can think of, and stay calm. You can't stay calm in yourself, but it's the peace of God that goes beyond our understanding. God gave me that peace. He not only gave me that peace but He also gave me a love for this man. I really loved him! That had to be God loving him through me because, in myself, I couldn't do that.

When I got ready to go, I said, "You know I really love you, and I'm praying for you."

Well, it just totally disarmed him. He knew that something had to be bigger than me to be able to tell him that. But it wasn't just something that I was trying to get on his good side, but it was true. God put a love in my heart for this man.

Then I said, "I'll be back tomorrow."

So when I went back the next day; this is the third day now, he didn't have any more to say. He had said it all he had poured it all out, now Jesus had something to say to him. The result was, he gave his heart to the Lord. He became a hard, determined, passionate worker in that whole part of the country for the Lord. The Lord called him into the ministry and really anointed him; and we ordained him in the ministry.

Unlikely Politician

In times past this political party of the government had been in office for years, and years, they called them the PUP. Here we have the Democrats and the Republicans; there they have the PUP, (Peoples United Party) and the UDP, (Untied Democratic Party). The PUP had been in power so long the people in all of that back woods area down in there had been totally neglected for years. So they felt like they needed to rise up and let their voice be heard. Now these Indian people that we had reached for Christ had never taken part in any kind of government affairs or their Nation's affairs; nothing like that, but something had happened to them, they were transformed.

Some of the officials began to ask, "Mr. Hooper, what are you doing to these people?"

"I'm not doing anything to them, I'm just telling them about Jesus and He's changing their lives," I would answer.

It wasn't just a change on the inside, they began to come out and take their place in the country.

So they began to come to this brother, and say, "We want you to run as a Representative for the UDP in the Toledo district."

Well, he never had thought about running for an office.

"I don't stand a chance against these Politicians; I've never done anything like that," he said.

"Would you please run and just give it a chance?" they asked him.

Do you know he won! God put him in that office. He began to represent them and later he was elevated in the government to the "Minister of Natural Resources" for the whole country of Belize. That was the one that Jesus loved. The Gospel has never lost its power. But we as witnesses need to be very careful how we present the Gospel. Jesus didn't come to condemn the world; He came to save, to seek and to save them. If we want to save people we're going to have to overlook the things that are in them at the present. We're going to need to understand that Jesus died for that person. That person right there that we're talking to, that we're witnessing to; Jesus died for them, and they are valuable to Him.

Love Restored

There was a love net knit together, from the day he quit regurgitating; till today. It's still there; I visited him not long ago. I was in Belize, and it's quite a journey way down to where he lives. When I go down there, there are so many places I need to go, I can't get to all of them sometimes, but I really felt like I needed to go see him.

The enemy had come against him in one of the hardest ways; and that is coming between him and his wife.

That's where the enemy can do a whole lot of damage. For a number of years; he lived upstairs and she lived downstairs.

If they wanted to talk to one another they would tell their son, "Go tell your mamma this, or go tell your daddy that."

My heart just cried, "Oh God do something in their marriage, I can't fix it."

We can't fix things, but we know the One who can. Jesus is real, He's alive, and He wants to do great things.

We kept praying, "God do something in their life."

When I walked up to his little porch he was lying in the hammock after lunch, relaxing. When he looked up and saw me, oh my goodness; he jumped straight up and ran as fast as he could to grab and hug me. I looked and there was his wife coming out the door to greet me.

I said, "Oh, hallelujah! Something's going on here!"

Something had gone on. The Lord had done so great a miracle in each one of them that brought them back together; and now they love each other and are happy together. It was wonderful, but it took an adversity. His wife got really sick. One of their son's grew up to become a pilot. He's a pilot in Belize, and flies for Tropic Air. When tourists go to Belize they have planes that take you out to Ambergris Caye, or the different islands and places.

When she was real sick he took the plane down to Punta Gorda, and took his mamma, flew her to Belize City; only to find out that what she had they could not help her.

They said, "You're going to have to go to Guatemala City, Mexico City, or the United States, or somewhere else, because we can't help you."

So she said, "Take me to Mexico City."

He couldn't fly her there in that plane, because their plane couldn't leave Belize. So they had to charter a plane. They chartered the plane, flew her to Mexico City; only to find out when they got there that they wouldn't admit her into that hospital because they didn't have the money. They had some money but they spent most of it getting her there. He had $300.00 left in his pocket, that's all he had. He had some other money, but it takes awhile to get money from Belize into US dollars and get it up there; and his wife needed immediate attention.

So he was crying out, "Oh God, do something. Help us some-way, do something for us. Help them to just accept this $300.00 or something just to get her admitted."

So he went to talk to the officials there at the hospital, "My wife needs attention now, she needs it right now and all I've got is this $300.00," he said.

He pulled it out to give it to them and it was $3,000.00! Three thousand dollars! Can God multiply? The same one that multiplied the loaves and the fishes; can He do that? Absolutely He can!

He was so happy about that; but he said, "I haven't told anybody about that because I know they wouldn't believe me, but I know you'll believe me."

While he was telling me tears were flowing down his face; and through all that the Lord brought him and his wife back together; and they love each other and are living happily. Praise God!

Don't give up if you're praying for your loved ones, or things that seem impossible, Don't give up because God is on the throne.

He is not going to be crowned one day, He is already crowned; "King of Kings and Lord of Lords." Hallelujah! He's our God. Praise God! He is our God!

The reason that God wants these things to be known is because we are His witnesses in the earth today. The enemy is out to kill, steal and destroy. He's trying to undermine Christianity, he's trying to undermine anything that is supernatural, or anything that God does. He doesn't want it to appear like a miracle; it's just one of those things that would have happened anyway. He's trying to deceive people. But we, who have been raised up for this generation; stand and declare the power of the living God.

So He said, "Put it in book form so that people can read it and be drawn to Me."

This is all about Jesus. He's the God of Jacob, and He is our God today.

Chapter 4

Steps of the Journey

Without a Vision, People Perish

It is such a joy to hear people testify. Each one of us has an experience that we can share with somebody else that will encourage their heart along this journey. We need each other, and it is real difficult to have a testimony without the test. If it was up to me, I'd leave off the test and just have the "mony."

So what I've developed in my life when I find myself going through a difficult test, my confession is, "I'm right in the middle of a brand new testimony."

The Lord is not going to leave us or forsake us but He is going to bring us through a brand new testimony. So it just thrills my heart to hear somebody testifying and sharing what God has done in their life. I believe God has something tremendous planned for our generation.

God is concerned. That is why Jesus left heaven and came to

earth; to seek and to save those that were lost. That's why He saved and called us to reach out to somebody else that is lost.

The heart of God is to go ye into all the world and preach, not a gospel; "The Gospel." *"the Gospel of Christ; for it is the power of God unto salvation to everyone that believeth"* (Rom. 1:16). *"You go,"* He said, *"and lo I will be with you."* (Matt. 28:19-20).

Somebody said, "No go--no lo."

We can't all go in person but we can go in prayer, in intercession, we can go in giving. We can go in different ways, but somebody has to put the leather on their feet and go.

I remember when the Lord began to call me, I told him about a whole bunch of preachers who could do a better job than me.

"Just let me stay here, work and support the Gospel," I answered.

But He didn't agree with that.

He said, "I want you!"

It's like that picture of Uncle Sam out in front of the Post Office; you don't see it much anymore, the caption read, "I want you."

That's what the Lord does; He lays his hand on us for His own purpose.

"Where there is no vision, the people perish" (Prov. 29:18).

Who was He talking to? I think He was talking to the church. I think He was talking to me! If I don't have a vision and I'm not reaching out, there are going to be people perish. I need to obey God and reach out since this is the very heart of God. At one time every one of us was lost and without Christ. Today we can sing and shout and remember the day and all that, but somehow the Lord reached us. He reached us, didn't He? He reached us so that we could reach out to somebody else.

God Gives a Vision

I was in a meeting in Guatemala. That's a little ways from Belize, and we often went over there and had meetings. They were singing and praising God in Spanish. I don't know a whole lot of Spanish, just a little bit, so I was just sitting there. Do you know what? I couldn't understand what they were saying but I could feel the presence of God. It doesn't matter what language you worship Him in He will receive it, and when His presence is there you just feel at home.

So I was sitting there just drinking in the presence of the Lord, and all of a sudden God caught me out in a trance. He showed me a whole lot of people in a huge pit, like an open mine pit. People were all over the place in this huge pit mingling around but there were no stairs, elevators, or any other way out of that pit. I remember walking around the walls of this pit looking up and looking around trying to find some way to get out of this pit. I saw that there were many others who were trying to get out, and there were many who were satisfied to remain in the pit.

While I was looking around I was wondering, "How am I ever going to get out of this pit?"

I looked and there was an arm; hand and arm, all the way up to the shoulder, reaching down to me. When this arm reached down to me I knew that was my way out! So this hand reached down to me and I clasped onto it, and this arm began to lift me up out of this pit. I looked back, and there was somebody looking up and looking for a way out, so I reached out my hand to them. I knew that the powerful arm that reached out to me could not only bring me out, but that other person as well. So they reached out to grab my hand and I could hardly wait to see who it was that reached out to me! When I got to the top and looked; all I could see was hands and arms linked all the way back to the cross!

Oh my, it did something to me. We are a link in that chain; from the cross to the lost. Are we not a part of that chain from the cross to the lost? Absolutely! Somebody reached out to us. Somebody prayed for us. Somebody believed for us, and while we were yet sinners Jesus died for us because He loves us.

My prayer is, "God, lay souls upon my heart. Never let me become satisfied with what I have accomplished or done, or been in my walk with the Lord. God, continue to put that burden for the souls of men, women, boys and girls upon my heart; because that's the compassion that will reach out to them."

The power of the Gospel has not diminished, *"it is [still] the power of God unto salvation to everyone that believeth,"* (Rom. 1:16); *"how shall they believe in Him on whom they have not heard? And how shall they hear without a preacher? And how shall they preach, except they be sent?"* (Rom. 10:14-15).

It is all a chain, isn't it? It's a chain that reaches clear back to the cross and reaches out to us. There are many lost people out there that need Jesus Christ. They don't need a program and they don't need a doctrine they need a revelation of Jesus! They need a touch, a personal touch of Jesus in their hearts and in their lives. I have never met a person that really met Jesus and was ever the same again. You just can't do it. Praise God!

Peace Passing Understanding

When we left Belize, I turned the leadership that the Lord had put into our hands to our son-in-law. He was a former alcohol and drug addict. There wasn't a moment of the day that he wasn't drinking alcohol or taking drugs, from the first thing when he got up in the morning. I knew him from the time he was a little boy; and watching him grow up that way, just burdened and grieved my heart.

I would pray, "God save him, get his attention, do something for him."

He was really big into the game they call football there. They call it football there but we call it soccer here. He was really big into that. We set up a volleyball net in the yard by the church and we would get some of the young people out there and play volleyball. We introduced volleyball to Belize.

He would pass by and we'd invite him to come and play with us; and he would say, "No, that's a sissy's game."

The real problem was, he didn't think he could play with us without cursing and carrying on, and didn't want to do that with a church group. But see, Peter used a net to catch fish, and we used a net, sometimes a volleyball net, to catch men. *"he who wins souls is wise"* (Prov. 11:30 NKJV). He kept coming by, and one day we coaxed him to come in.

He came in to play and God got his attention. He saved and totally transformed him into a brand new creation from the inside out. He would sit on the front seat of the church attentive to every word. The scene reminded me of a hungry baby bird with his beak open, waiting for his next morsel. He was that hungry for God's Word. When I would go out he would want to go with me and be a part of the services in other places; and in the process of time, he became a minister and married our baby daughter. We had gotten him appointed as a "Marriage Officer." They became the leaders of what God has been doing in Belize.

Years later the Lord sent me back up to the United States. About a year and a half after that, they were coming home from a wedding. He had officiated at the wedding ceremony. Our daughter had written the song for the new couple, sang it, and gave it to the bride. She was killed on the way home in a head-on collision with a drunk driver. There are some things that we just cannot understand.

I'll never forget when they called me about 3:00 o'clock in the morning, "Brother Samuel, your daughter is dead," they said.

She was expecting a baby and they both were killed instantly.

I felt like Jacob when they told him that Joseph had been killed. The Bible says that he could not be comforted. That's the way I felt. It felt like nobody could say anything that would comfort my heart. I just could *not* be comforted. She was a toddler when we went to Belize, less than 3 years old. She was raised there, and graduated from being a missionary's daughter to a missionary. She was a soul winner and a tremendous musician, talented singer, and song writer.

She wrote several songs about Belize that became some of their national songs.

I couldn't understand, "Why would you take her, Lord? There are so many lazy people out there who don't want to do anything; and we need workers in the field."

I just couldn't be comforted. Our son and his wife, my sister and her husband, from Hot Springs, AR were visiting us and we were all in the living room. Somebody said, "Maybe we ought to pray." I could not pray. I couldn't say anything. I just felt so crushed inside. Then our son cried out loudly, "OH GOD, PLEASE HELP US, WE'RE HURTING!"

The peace of God came in that room and settled over all of us; and God gave me His peace. Now the Bible says that the peace of God goes beyond our understanding. You can't analyze it, but it comes from Him. He brings that peace into our heart.

Our daughter and the baby she was expecting were both killed. She left behind one son. We have one grandson, and we just appreciate him so much.

It took them hours to get our son-in-law out of the vehicle. They took him to the hospital, but they gave him up for dead, and he laid there unconscious for days. While he was lying unconscious in the hospital, they buried his wife and our daughter. I have never seen any two people that loved each other more than they did. He never got to say goodbye and it really just devastated him.

While he was unconscious in the hospital, his soul was in heaven and the Lord asked him, "Do you want to go back or do you want to come here with me?"

"Lord, your will be done," he said.

The Lord raised him up.

He was in the hospital in Belize. They worked with him there, and he was having terrible pain in his neck. They couldn't do anything more for him, so they sent him to the hospital in Guatemala City to see if they could help him there.

He walked into that hospital and they X-rayed him.

"How did you get here?" they inquired.

"Well, I walked in here," he answered.

His neck was broken in four places but he was still alive!

They said, "We're going to have to do this, and this, and this."

"It doesn't make any difference, do what you need to do. If you need to take my head clear off you can't kill me; because I would have already been dead if God wanted me dead," he replied.

A Leader in Belize

God raised him up and restored his health. A man nobody knew previously has been raised up by God to be a tremendous leader with the Government and the School officials in the country of Belize.

Several years later the Lord blessed him with another wife who loves the Lord. They go out into the schools, testify and share the Gospel with the young people, and teach them the ways of God. They meet with the Government leaders in Belize on television and radio.

God has begun to use him now in a Soccer team. He became a coach of a little young team there on the mission compound. He would work with them and talk with them, and they have now won all the trophies of Belize, the trophies in Mexico and all the trophies in the Dominican Republic! He's reaching not only these young men, but he's reaching their parents and the Government officials.

When they came back from the Dominican Republic with the golden crown, there were people all over the place. There was the news media, the ministers of Government, and hundreds of people there to welcome them back! Nothing had ever happened like that before in the country of Belize, and this is the Christian team. I want to tell you, God knows how to reach the souls of people if we would just be wise.

He called me the other day and was so excited, "I can't under-stand how I got to this place, and how God has done these great things; I can't understand it," he said.

"I do, you just let the Lord use you," I said.

All God wants is a vessel, just a willing vessel. He's going to do the work.

Farmer Missionaries

When the Lord really dealt with me to go to Belize, I didn't want to go. I was Pastoring a church in Arizona and you never knew what God was going to do. People were afraid to miss a service because God always did something, and did it different. Right in the middle of all that the Lord asked me to go to Belize. I did not want to go. I didn't know anybody there. I wasn't looking for excitement or a thrill. I just wanted to obey God.

God said to me, "I want to go to Belize." Then He said, "Will you go with me?"

Do you know why He wanted me to go there? Because there were souls there that He loved. I didn't love them, because I didn't even know them, but He loved them. He sent me there to preach the Gospel of Christ, the Good News. I tell you, it's Good News!

They wouldn't even let us in the country as missionaries, so we had to go as "Experimental Farmers." That was the truth because I had never done any farming before. So we became "Experimental Farmers."

We planted Kentucky Wonder beans and they outgrew the bean stalks. The carrots we planted got a foot long. We planted some Longhorn okra, and we had to take a ladder to get up to it. God blessed those plants that we planted out there by the road.

One day one of the Government officials came by and stopped to look.

"You know, you're really the kind of people we want here in this country," he said.

People would go down there and buy land for an investment, but they wouldn't develop it.

So it was my chance, and I don't ever miss a chance to share Jesus; so I said, "Really sir, I appreciate the compliment, but that is really not what I came here for."

So I told him why I came.

"I can't really do what God sent me here to do without the permission from your Government. I need my immigration status changed from an 'Experimental Farmer' to a 'Minister of Religion,'" I said.

That's what they call it there.

"You come in the office and we'll see what we can do," he replied.

When God is in a thing He makes it work! I went into their office and told them that we came there not just to plant vegetables and raise chickens, but to help people find Jesus. When they find Jesus they change, and they change for the good.

"We're going to give you the 'Minister of Religion' authority, but you can still farm and raise chickens and crops also," they said.

God knew that we had to have that authority from the Government to be able to do what He sent us there to do.

Up here they call it planting churches. Down there it's pioneering churches, because there isn't anything there. You start from scratch and you just start telling them about Jesus. We would drive up and down the highway; and the highways aren't anything like they are here. We had two large 21" speakers, one on the front of the truck and one on the back, and we played gospel music going down the road. They could hear us coming for 3 miles and hear us after we passed for 3 miles. If we found anyone along the road we'd stop and tell them about Jesus and give them a tract. Whenever we found a village we pulled in there, got the mike stand out, put the mike in it and started sharing Jesus with the people. Many times we didn't see anyone but they were there.

So we preached to "nothing," and just do it over and over, sometimes 15 times a day; just sharing Jesus, preaching the Gospel. Hallelujah!

Sometimes it looked like we weren't accomplishing anything but we didn't look at what it looked like. I found out faith is going on no matter what it looks like or how you feel about it. Then God began to work.

God Supplies All Needs

We went there by faith.

God said, "Go."

He is big enough to supply all my needs, or else I can't trust Him with my eternal soul. That's the way I look at it. So we didn't go around itinerating, raising money, and getting people to promise to send so much. We just went, us and our four children. The Lord would speak to somebody's heart in the states to send us an offering. There wasn't any money there and we couldn't work there so we trusted God. God would begin to send it in time and time again as it was needed.

People would write to me and ask, "Brother Sam, what do you need there in Belize?"

I would answer, "We need a Holy Ghost revival!"

"Yeah, I know that, but what do you really need?" they would ask.

I said, "We need a Holy Ghost revival!"

We needed a Holy Ghost revival because the country was in total darkness. When it came to the power of God, they had no knowledge of that. There was an organization in the western part of the country that was called "Pentecostal," but there was nothing there. It was dried up on the vine.

So it was total darkness. But I want you to know that; *"greater is He that is in you, [us] than he that is in the world"* (1 John 4:4).

We knew we had to stand strong in the Lord and be faithful. So we just kept going, and going. You know, God supplied us with every means of transportation we needed. He gave us an airplane and two boats. He gave us a motorcycle, four-wheel drive trucks; and if we couldn't get there any other way, we walked. So we got there and spread the Gospel all over that country.

We didn't back up, we didn't get defeated, we didn't get discouraged. We just obeyed God and took the Gospel to the people. Not them coming to us, we took it to them. After a period of time, just being faithful, pounding on a rock, with the Lord's help we broke through.

The Bible says that the Word of God is *"like a hammer that breaketh the rock in pieces"* (Jer. 23:29).

You don't break the rock the first time you hit it, you've got to keep hitting it. Anybody that knows about rock work knows that you have got to keep hitting that rock; and after awhile it'll crack and it will break.

I'm not in any way boasting on us, I'm boasting on Jesus! Jesus is the same today as He ever has been. We read about the Apostles going from place to place and village to village. Some places they would receive them gladly, and other times they would stone them or kick them out. We've had some of those same experiences; but the Gospel will prevail. If we want God's blessings in our life today, let's get involved in what God's heart is, and it's to reach out to the lost. As surely as God saved us, He wants to use us to reach out to somebody else. Anyway we can do it, we're going to do it, and we are going to believe God.

The Lord never failed. There were times when we needed to build a tabernacle. We didn't go build churches and then invite people to come. We built the church and let them be a part of the building. We would need a little tabernacle where they could meet out of the rain or sunshine. I would go to the saw mill, because they don't have lumber yards there; they just have a saw mill way out in the jungle. I would go and order what lumber we needed to build a tabernacle. They never questioned me because down in Belize all

Americans are rich. So they would never question me, but when I would order the lumber, I didn't have the money to pay for it. There was not a time, not one single time; when they wrote and told me the lumber was ready, that God didn't provide. When it came in I always had the money to pay for it.

One time God told me to order a 50 horsepower Mercury engine for our speed boat that we used to get to villages that we couldn't get to any other way.

I said, "But God that cost a lot of money."

"You go order it," He replied.

So I went to the Mercury dealership in Belize City. It so happened that the owner had attended a huge tent revival that we had in Belize City, and knew me. I didn't really know him, but he knew me.

He said, "Oh, yeah, you are preacher Hooper, aren't you?"

"Well yes, I need a 50 horsepower Mercury engine. Do you have one?" I asked.

"No I don't, and it will take about 3 months to get one," he replied.

"Order it," I said, and then I asked, "How much do I need to pay?"

"Oh no, you don't have to pay anything. When it comes in you can pay for it," he answered.

Now it was getting close for the 3 months to be up; and it was about time for the engine to come in, and I didn't have the money to pay for it.

"Now Lord, You've never failed yet and here we're getting close," I said.

One day I went to the Post Office and there in the mail was this huge check from a man that had promised God three years before that he was going to send money to help with the ministry in Belize. He promised the Lord and he hadn't done it. Now he couldn't get by anymore, so he obeyed God and sent it. It was exactly what I needed to pay for the boat engine!

I'm telling you, we lived there for 29 years strictly by faith. We never wrote a newsletter saying we need this, or we need something else. God always provided. I have learned that God's work, done in God's way, will never lack God's provision.

God raised up many churches in Belize. In some of the villages the whole village would accept Christ. One thing we needed the airplane for was; we lived in the western district, and there were a lot of rivers that get flooded between us and the southern part of the country. Sometimes it would take several hours; sometimes it would take many days to get there. With this little airplane we could be there in 20 minutes.

There were so many people getting married that they had me going back and forth quite a lot. Most of the people just lived together before being born again. We have had Grandchildren attend their Grandparent's weddings. When they knew Jesus, nobody told them they had to do this or that. They automatically wanted to get their lives straightened out, so they wanted to get married. Well since I was the only "Marriage Officer" at that time, they really kept me busy; but it was a good busy. We were seeing people becoming established in the Lord and in a good life.

God Himself would raise up leadership in every single village. He would lay His hand upon people for the Pastoral work, the Elders, and so forth. He would raise up the leadership. Then we would work with them. Share with them, testify with them, teach them, and take them to different churches; and let God work in their lives. God's way is the best way, and it's a beautiful way. Oh, Hallelujah!

An Airplane Given

I have always liked flying, but I never thought that we would ever have an airplane on the mission field. I was surprised at how many people didn't like that idea.

"Missionaries shouldn't have an airplane," they would say.

That was back years ago, but God knew what we needed.

So the Lord caused a brother to come down and see what we were doing; and he said, "You need an airplane here."

I said, "Well yeah, but they are expensive and cost money to operate."

"I believe the Lord can handle that," he said.

So he took it on his heart to look around and finally found one that had been used in Guatemala as a missionary aircraft.

He purchased it for twelve thousand dollars and brought it over to us. "Here," he said.

Now, I like flying, and I had done some flying with my uncle when I was younger; but I was in no condition to fly that airplane around, because you fly by the seat of your pants. You don't have any radar or anything else.

So we said, "Well now Lord we need a pilot."

God sent us a pilot; a young man that loved God, full of zeal. He came down there just to be our pilot, and take us where ever we needed to go. He wound up falling in love with our oldest daughter and married her. After the Wedding they lived in Texas. So the mission work in Belize lacked our pilot and daughter both.

A New Pilot

Now, where do we go from there? We had met a fellow on one of the islands out in the Caribbean Sea that was a flight instructor.

He said, "I'll teach you."

Of course we had flown a lot in Belize, and I could tell you about all kinds of experiences we had; but I didn't have a license.

So he said, "I can help you get your license."

The flight out to the island where he lived was beautiful. The big coral reef of that country is absolutely gorgeous. We began flying;

and oh my goodness, he put me through the drill. He had me flying 50 feet off of the water. Now look, 50 feet isn't very high when you're up in an airplane. The wheels are even almost touching the water, if that plane even coughs; you're in the water. Then he had me doing climbing stalls, until it stalled out, and that buzzer would come on and that thing was yelling, and the plane would fall. Now you've got to be able to recover it quickly. He's teaching you all that because if you come in to land and hit a downdraft or something, and loose control; you've got to get it back quick. Gliding stalls, climbing stalls; all kind of things he put me through.

"Oh my God, I didn't know there was so much involved in flying," I said.

An Aircraft Lost

Anyway, we were getting along real good. We were having a huge conference and tent meeting in Belize City. We would fly over the city and surrounding villages dropping leaflets that would announce the dates, times and place of the meetings. We had installed a Mid-America STOL kit and other improvements on this aircraft after it was given to the ministry. That STOL kit enabeled the plane to get in and out of short runways.

It was during this tent crusade that the gentleman that had purchased the plane showed up, "I've come to get the aircraft," he said.

Still in shock, I asked, "You're doing what?"

Then he said again, "I came to get the aircraft."

I asked him, "Brother, do you remember what you said? You gave this plane to the work of God here. We all gathered around the plane and dedicated this aircraft to the work of God here in Belize."

"Yeah, I remember that, but I've come to get the plane," he replied.

At that time we were flying the airplane out of a small dirt runway at the Belize City airport, and that's where it was.

"All the paperwork on the plane is at my house 60 miles from here, we'll have to fly out there and get it," I said.

You can't fly a plane without all the paperwork being exact and we had just gone through it and redid it. I was flying back to our place with this gentleman that was going to fly it back to the states. He and his associates were in the business of teaching missionaries to fly a plane; and helping them get a plane on the mission field.

He said to me, "Brother Samuel, I don't know why this man wants to take this plane off of the mission field, because we are doing our best to teach young men how to fly, and put planes on the mission field. He is giving me this plane, I don't know why; but if I have anything to do with it, this aircraft will come back to Belize."

That evening we flew out to our house and soon after that it was dark. We had made arrangements with the gentleman to meet him and his wife the next morning at the International Airport at Belize City.

That night in prayer the Lord spoke to me and said, "He's taking this airplane out of My will," just as clear as could be.

The next morning we got the papers. The gentleman that was going to fly the plane was with me and we flew back to the International Airport at Belize City. When we got back to the airport this man and his wife were waiting there.

"Brother, I'm not going to tell you what to do; but I'm going to tell you what God told me," I said.

He said, "You're taking this aircraft out of God's will."

His wife began to cry, "Honey, don't do this," she begged.

But he replied sternly, "I'm doing it anyway."

He carried out his plan and took it. Sad to say; not too long after that, in his own garage in south Texas, he was bitten by a rattle snake and died. It's a serious thing to give something to God and then take it back, it's serious.

Just Jesus and Me

Well then, this man began to teach me in his airplane. Ours was a Cessna 180 with Cleveland brakes and wheels, a STOL kit and all that. Now when I started flying this little 150, it would just bounce around, little bitty thing; it was like you would get out of a big ol' Cadillac and get in a little bitty VW bug. So I had a difficult time learning, because I had to start all over in this little plane. I remember we were way down south, had a dirt field there, and we were doing "touch and go" landings. For those of you who don't know what that is: you come in, you've got your throttle down; your heat on your carburetor, got your flaps down, and all that, and you touch on the runway; then you take that all off and get back up off the runway, before you hit the trees on the other end.

My instructor said, "Sam, this next round, just stop and I'm going to get out."

I asked, "You're going to what?"

"Yeah, I'm going to get out," he replied.

"Are you sure?" I inquired. "This is your airplane and if I wreck it I don't have the money to pay for it."

He said, "I'm sure. If I wasn't sure, I wouldn't tell you to let me out."

I'll never forget when I let him out and took off of that runway; and got back up in the sky.

"Lord, It's just You and me now," I said.

There is no feeling quite like it. I was flying around over the land and the Caribbean Sea and everything.

He once told me, "I want you to do some of these "touch and go" landings."

Well you've got to get the carburetor heat on, the throttle down, the flaps down; and everything has all got to happen at the same time as you're coming in. As you're coming down that ground gets real close to you before you touch it, I mean its right there. You've got to touch it on the end of the landing strip too, if you're going to get off of the other end of it without hitting the trees.

"Jesus, it's me and You," I said.

I touched that thing down, and as I touched the wheels down, I waved at him, and pushed the throttle on, pushed the carburetor heat off; pulled the flaps off, and up I went.

And said, "Thank you Jesus; thank you Jesus!"

Crashed Plane

Now I'll tell you some flying stories. With that same aircraft, the Cessna 180, we were having a camp meeting in Arkansas. We had a camp meeting there and people came from many states. Some had never been to a camp meeting. The Lord put it on our hearts to do that; so we rented a big camp ground, and just had several days of camp meeting. People from other states went back from there and started camp meetings in their church area. Actually, our daughter and son-in-law, my pilot, got married in that camp meeting. After we had finished that camp meeting, we had a big bus that we had loaded with all kinds of things we were taking back to Belize.

Somebody had given us a real nice Onan generator, because for many years we had no electricity in Belize. We didn't even have an inside restroom. We had a little house out back, and had a water vat we caught water off the roof to take a bath in. So whatever temperature the water was, that's what you bathed in, and no generator. So somebody had given us a generator and different things for the work there.

We had flown the plane to the camp meeting in Arkansas. We were going to do some work on it, and get it up to specks and everything.

When it came time to go, one of the brothers that was in the camp meeting said, "I'm a pilot, I cut my teeth on tail draggers."

If you know anything about a 180; it's a tail dragger. It has a rear wheel instead of a nose wheel. You've got to fly that thing from the time you get it going until it stops. It's not like the nose wheel, you kind of drive it. So he was bragging about how he could fly this plane.

"I cut my teeth on tail draggers," he said.

We were working on the bus, getting last minute things done, and my son-in-law went with this brother out to the airport in Hot Springs, Arkansas to check him out and see if he could really fly it. Did you know he ground looped that aircraft? On a runway that we could have landed on going sideways! He let it get away from him, and it turned sideways and the landing gear buckled underneath the aircraft. So it tore up the wings, the tail, the prop; and everything on the aircraft. He was really helpful; he got out of it and walked off and left it sitting right there.

Airplane Repairs

Now those are some of the trials and tests that I would like to go around. We were just getting ready to go back to Belize.

It takes a lot of money to fix an airplane when something like this happens, so my heart was just crushed; but I said, "God, Romans 8:28 is still true; *"And we know that all things work together for good to them that love God (You), to them who are the called according to His (Your) purpose."*

I knew a man over in Tennessee that rebuilt aircraft, he used to live in Arkansas, so I called him up.

I said, "Brother; such and such has happened."

Oh he felt so bad, "Just take the wing off put it on a trailer; bring it over here, and I'll fix it," he said.

But I knew he was covered up in work and it would take so long to get it done; and I just didn't want to impose on him.

"Well Brother; could you just tell me somewhere around here that could repair the wing? We could take it off and take it there and get it repaired; and maybe the propeller," I inquired.

So he told us about a certain man in Oklahoma who could fix the wing. So we took it off and made a framework out of some 2 x 4's on the back of a pickup and strapped that wing onto it. We had just gone through Mena, Arkansas and had just barely got into the edge of Oklahoma; at a little one horse town, I call it; and stopped at a 7-11 to get some gas and use the restroom and met a man there. I went to the restroom and came out and saw our pilot and new son-in-law talking to this man around the magazine rack.

He was looking at flying magazines, and asked him, "Is that your wing out there on that truck?"

"Yeah, it is," he replied.

He inquired, "Well, what happened?"

So he told him how the aircraft was wrecked.

About that time I came out there, and said, "We're on our way to see this certain man here in Oklahoma. They tell us that he can fix this wing, but we have a question; because on this aircraft we had installed a Mid-America STOL kit; and that's to be able to get in and out of short field landings, and we don't know if he knows how to repair that STOL kit."

The man looked at us and started grinning.

"You are not going to believe this; but I helped design and engineer that Mid-America STOL kit you've got on that airplane," he said.

Can you believe that? I mean, way out in the middle of nowhere. When he said that something just leaped inside of me!

"Well maybe you could help us fix it?" I asked.

"I sure will! You be at the airport in the morning at 8:00 o'clock, and I'll help you. I'll put you to drilling rivets, and we'll get that thing fixed," he said.

Free Parts

There was only one little motel in that town. It wasn't very fancy, but it had beds in it. In the night, while we were sleeping in that motel, I had a dream. In this dream I saw that this man we had talked to, invited us home with him for supper; and when he did, God saved him. God saved him! This was in my dream. At 8:00 o'clock the next morning we were out at the airport. We started drilling out rivets and everything.

We told him, "You know, there's some airplane wrecking yards over in Mena, Arkansas. We're going to drive over there and see if we can get parts to repair this plane."

"Just take my little 150 and fly over there," he said.

Now, we don't know this guy. Our plane had been wrecked and now he's going to let us use his plane? That's God!

I said, "Well sir, I really appreciate that, but if we get the parts we need, we can't bring them back in that little 150."

"Well, I see your point," he replied.

So we took off in the pickup, and while we were driving along; I said to our son-in-law, "Let me tell you something. When we get back this afternoon, and this gentleman invites us home for supper; he's a saved man. Yeah, that's going to be the sign."

We got over to Mena and went to this big wrecking yard. We went into the hanger and this guy was up on a big, high ladder, working on the nose of a big twin engine aircraft.

I introduced myself, "We're looking for a Cessna wing, and we need some parts off of it," I said.

"Just go out there and look and see if you find anything," he said.

We went out there and found a whole wing, just exactly what we needed!

But I thought, "Well my goodness, how can we afford to buy this?"

We went back in, and inquired, "We found a Cessna wing out there, but how much do you want for it?"

He wanted to know, "Do you need the lights?"

"No, our lights are okay," I answered.

"Just take the blankety-blank thing and get out of here!" he said. "Just take the lights off, bring them in here, and just take it on."

I was dazed, you know; God even blesses us through sinners. That's right, they don't even know what they're doing; but it was God. I didn't ask him for it, I just ask him how much he wanted for it.

So we took the lights off and took them back in and he said, "Just don't tell anybody where you got it."

"But I *am* going to tell somebody," I said.

He looked at me with a scowl on his face.

"Yeah, I'm going to tell the Lord where I got it and ask Him to bless you!" I said.

He didn't quite know how to handle that.

We went over to the next wrecking yard. We needed some parts for the landing mechanisms, and went over there.

They said, "Just go out there, see what you can find, and when you find something; we've got tools here, take it off, lay it here, and when you get all done; we'll settle up."

So we did. We found quite a lot of parts that we needed there.

We brought them in, made the pile there, and asked them, "How much now for all these parts?"

They looked at them and at us and said, "Just take them on and use 'em."

I'm telling you; we've got a great big wonderful God. If the enemy tries to rob us; God will give it back. And that devil will wish he had never touched us. That's the way he feels, when God turns it around and works it out for our good; and he gets the black eye.

Then he says, "I should have left them alone."

So we had all this stuff loaded up in the truck. We had thousands of dollars worth of parts, and it didn't cost a thing!

A Marriage Healed

We got back about 4:00 o'clock in the afternoon.

Our new gentleman friend came down, looked in the truck, and said, "My goodness sakes. Y'all really got us some stuff. What did all that set you back?"

I answered, "Nothing."

"What?" he asked.

"Not a thing; not a thing," I said.

He was flabbergasted he didn't know what to say.

So he said this, "I was sure hoping you'd get back here; because my wife is cooking supper for you tonight."

I'm telling you, I almost went into orbit!

"Uh-huh, you are a saved man," I thought to myself.

So we replied, "Yeah, we'll be glad to have supper with you."

When we got to their house his wife was fixing a nice meal. We met her and the two young boys and sat down to a nice dinner together. It turned out that this gentleman had been through the war in Viet Nam and came home all torn to pieces; like many did that came back from that war. He was a helicopter pilot over there.

Anyway, after we got through eating, he and my son-in-law went into the living room. They began to talk about airplanes, flying and all of that stuff. His wife and I were in the kitchen talking and she began to cry.

"I'm sure glad y'all came tonight; because I am going tomorrow to file for a divorce. I can't handle it anymore. I have done everything. I quit going to church and went to the taverns with him. I've done everything I could to save our marriage; but I can't handle it anymore," she said.

So, as I listened my heart just went out to her.

Finally, I said to her, "You have left out the only One who can help you. You've left Jesus out of your life, and He's the only One who can help."

Now, I already knew that the Lord was going to save her husband, but I didn't tell her that. I knew he was already had, God had his number; but I didn't want to tell her that. I wanted her to make herself right with God. So after a little bit, we prayed together. She began to ask the Lord to forgive her for leaving Him out of her life. She just poured out her heart, and the Lord joyously forgave her. The joy came back into her heart and she was so excited.

That is what God can do, I mean in a few minutes time. He can take that heavy burden, and turn it around into His glorious presence; *"beauty for ashes, the oil of joy for mourning, the garment of praise for the spirit of heaviness"* (Isa. 61:3).

We sat there then and began to fellowship, and about midnight the other two men came back into the kitchen. She excused herself, did the dishes, and went to bed. I knew the Lord was going to save this man; but I'm telling you what, he was a hard nut to crack. I'd say something to him, and he'd come back at me with a hard answer. I'd share something else with him, and he'd come back with another hard answer. That went on until 3:00 o'clock in the morning! Had God not given me that promise, I might have kind of faltered, but I never faltered, and I didn't allow him to offend me.

He couldn't understand why I would not get offended, because he hit me with some hard things. He had bitterness inside of him, and it was coming out; and he was using it on me. I know it wasn't just him; because he was a kind man, but it was the enemy. Satan was determined he was going to hold onto that soul and destroy that home; and I was determined he wasn't, and I didn't let go! I was like a bull dog that had hold of a throat, and I did not let go. No matter what he said, I didn't get offended.

Just in my heart I kept saying, "Thank you Lord he's a saved man."

At 3:00 o'clock in the morning, he finally bowed his head, repented, and gave his heart to Jesus. At 3:00 o'clock in the morning, God saved their souls and their family! They're still serving God and still together. Hallelujah!

"Well, it was worth it all for the plane to get wrecked to save this soul, this family and these lives," I said.

So the brother said, "It's too late to go back to that old motel, just make the couch out into a bed, and you can rest there."

When we got up the next morning, he said, "Sam, I'm not going to tell anybody what happened to me last night."

Now, he's a big shot out at their airport, he is the A & E and A & I inspector.

I looked right at him and said, "Man, if you can keep it to yourself, more power to you."

I didn't tell him, "Hey, you've got to witness."

No, you know when God really does something you can't keep it to yourself, you just absolutely can't. So sure enough; when we got out there, he could hardly get out until he started telling everybody. It took a long time to get that plane fixed because it was always like a revival going on. I want to tell you; God is in charge, but our attitude has a whole lot to do with the outcome of the situation. We've got to hold on, we've got to believe, and see God work the salvation of souls. Praise God!

First Flight to Belize

We were on our way to Belize the first time in a little aircraft, a 1948 Stinson. It was a four place plane; but let me tell you, it was a crowded four place plane; we had to sit sideways in the back seat. We were flying from Globe, Arizona; going to Belize, after God had spoken to us. We went down to check out what we needed to take and kind of observe what was going on. There were four of us in this plane. We intended to fly all the way to Minatitlan, Mexico; where there was a beautiful group that was really on fire for God. We were going to be in service and stay all night with them that night. The plan went real good going along in Mexico. We were flying 10,500 feet over those mountain peaks, and then there were times when it felt like the wheels were going to touch the tree tops. There were other times when you'd look down and the houses would look like little specks.

I'll never forget flying over there I began to weep.

"God, how many people down there really know you? How many have ever been introduced to you?" I thought.

It was just the cry for souls.

About 20 minutes before we were to reach our destination, we met a tropical storm coming off the Gulf of Mexico. It was raining so hard, you couldn't see anything. There's such a thing as vertigo in an aircraft when you can't see anything, and you can't get your balance. You don't know if you're flying upside down, straight up or down; you don't know. You have got to trust the instruments, and this pilot didn't have all that much instrument training.

So we were flying into that thinking maybe we would just fly on through it pretty soon, but we didn't, it just kept persisting. So we had to turn around, do a 180, and come back the way we had been flying. Now we are in unfamiliar territory. All we have to fly by is a little chart that will show you a railroad, or a village or something like that. That's the way you fly; by the seat of your pants.

Now, whenever you're trusting the instruments it is almost like trusting the Lord, because it doesn't seem like they're doing right, it seems like they're all out of kilter. You don't feel like they're showing you the right thing, and that's when you've got to trust the instruments. I want to tell you, when we're going through things in this life and we don't feel like God is there; or we don't feel like things are going right, we have to *"Trust in the Lord with all thine (our) heart, and lean not unto thine own understanding"* (Prov. 3:5).

So we turned back and headed in the opposite direction. After awhile we got out of the rain storm. We had two gas tanks on that aircraft, but our gas gages read almost empty, and it's getting dark. Now in this chart it shows a railroad going into these three little villages. So before the sun went down, we were following this little railroad. The map showed that there was a landing strip somewhere in that area. When the sun goes down in the south it gets dark quick. It is against the law to fly in Mexico after dark, because they have these high radio towers with no lights on them. Pilots can't see the towers and planes crash. So they passed a law, but when you're up there you've got to get down; and if it gets dark on you, you're flying after dark.

A Promise

Now, back up just a little bit. We had stopped a little before that on a crop-dusting landing strip. They sold us five gallons of gas and poured it in out of a can.

While we were sitting there waiting on them to put the gas in, there was a little voice that spoke to me, and said, "The next time you're on the ground, you're going to be mighty glad to see it."

Well those are the kind of voices you don't want to hear when you're flying; no, it doesn't sound good at all.

So I rebuked the enemy. I said, "Get behind me Satan."

Now they told us how to fly down this mountain range and follow the river that cut through it. You could cut through the river bed, and that was real tricky. So when we were flying down that river bed to get out into the valley, the voice came to me again with the same words; I rebuked it.

Now, we have turned around, we're flying, the gas gages are getting close to empty, and the sun is going down. We can't see; we don't know where the village is, or where the landing strip is, and that little voice spoke to me again with those words. Do you know what I did?

I reached out and grabbed hold of it with both hands because it was a promise, "The next time you're on the ground, you're going to be mighty glad to see it!"

It was a promise, and all the time I was pushing it out.

So for the first time, I told the other brothers, "This is what this voice has been telling me all the time, I didn't want to believe it, but now I realize, it's a promise. We are going to be safely on the ground and we're going to be mighty glad to see it, so we are going to be alright!"

So in a little bit, both of the gas gages were bouncing on empty and we still weren't there. But, thank you Lord; when God gives you a promise reach out and hold onto it with both hands. Circumstances will make it look impossible, but God is the God of impossibilities.

So we prayed, and asked the Lord, "Now God, where is this landing strip in this area?"

One of the brothers said, "Brother, I feel like it's over here on the right."

Okay, so the pilot veers to the right and we get down as low as we dare because we don't know where the radio tower is. The pilot turned on our landing lights and when we flew over, we saw something that looked like it could be a landing strip. So, he banked that plane hard as he could, came back in a little bit lower with the landing lights on, and sure enough, it was a landing strip. So we flew on to the other end, banked it hard and landed. When we got out of that aircraft, we knelt down, gave the Lord thanks, and kissed the ground!

You know when you're sharing things like this it's not the same as it really feels like when you're going through it, but God's Word says to trust in Him. The Lord kept that plane flying. He didn't let it hit anything; no radio towers or anything like that, because; He said, "*In all your ways acknowledge Him, and He shall direct your paths*" (Prov. 3:6 NKJV).

The testimonies like we read of in the Bible are still being written. We read many of the testimonies of people and call their names; but there are some testimonies that God is writing down, that will be under our name one day when the books are opened and read. There will be your name and the times that God moved and worked;

answered prayer and used you and spoke through you; and you obeyed Him and did what He said. The book of Acts is still being written because it is the acts of the Holy Ghost; still being written. Hallelujah!

If you're in a commercial plane and the thing is going down, God can touch it too. That's right, because He is with His children. Why do things happen? Sometimes things happen because we don't reach out and touch God, we just let them happen. But God says, *"Resist the devil, and he will flee from you"* (James 4:7). If you are submitted to God, and resisting the devil, he will have to flee; he will have to get his dirty, rotten, stinking hands off of you!

Chapter 5

Our God Is Real

God Is Faithful

God is just as real when we don't feel Him, as when we do. He never goes up and down like a yo-yo, but we do, don't we? Part of the time we're up, and part of the time we're down, but He is always there. Isn't that wonderful?

So the Lord told me several years ago, "You just practice acknowledging My presence."

Practice is doing something over and over and over.

He said, "You practice that, because when I told you that I would never leave you and never forsake you, that is what I meant. So no matter how you feel, I'm still there. When you acknowledge My presence, then you will begin to feel My presence." Hallelujah!

Our daughter lives in a mobile home behind our house. She is fifty something years old and single. Her ministry is with God all the time, in intercession. The Lord takes her different places, and shows her the needs of different people; and what's going on in this country and that country. That is a much needed ministry in the body of Christ.

She was feeling really down the other day, she just felt like the Lord had forgotten about her.

"God, I've been faithful to do what you've asked me to do. I've tried to work, but it doesn't work, because You gave me a job and I'm working for You," she said.

Yet her financial supply had run down and she couldn't even pay her bills.

She felt like, "God, you've just kind of forsaken me, disappointed me and let me down."

I'm sure there are times when all of us kind of feel like, "Well, where are You, Lord?"

You know, my heart just went out to her, and there wasn't a whole lot I could say to her; because she has known God from the time she was a very little girl. She knows the Scriptures. She knows all these things, but it doesn't matter how much we know sometimes, the enemy attacks you with everything he can find to put on you. When he gets you to feeling like God has forsaken you he just really pushes on you then.

I had been praying, "God do something for her."

While we were sitting there enjoying a time of fellowship together, she received a call from the Lindale State Bank.

"There has been an anonymous donor that has just put $500.00 in your account, and we just wanted to call to let you know that it's there. If you didn't know it was there you wouldn't be able to use it," the lady said.

When we feel that God has just kind of forgotten about us, He hasn't forgotten at all. That news began to lift her out of that place of disappointment. It began to meet some of her needs, but it did more than that; it began to manifest to her that God is faithful. No matter what it looks like, God is faithful. Not, He used to be, but He is at this present time.

I'm telling you; it just lifted my spirit to know that God would manifest Himself to her in such a way that she could know that He is right there with her, no matter how she feels. A few years ago she came through cancer. She had a really bad case of ovarian cancer. There was really no hope for her, but the Lord brought her through; delivered her, and now she's cancer free. Praise God! Hallelujah!

The Greatest Miracle

I believe that the greatest miracle of all is the salvation of a lost soul. That is the greatest miracle of all.

When Jesus said, *"greater works than these shall he do"* (John 14:12).

Then we're trying to figure out how can we do greater than walking on the water, feeding five thousand with a little, and raising the dead? That's what He did, and I'm sure many things He did are not recorded in the Bible. Now how can we do greater than that? But Jesus had not died yet. His blood had not been sprinkled on the altar in heaven. The way of salvation had not been made yet. What He was talking about; "greater things," is that we have the Gospel that can transform people's lives. We have the greater thing. To see the transformation of a life that is steeped in sin and has been that way for years and years is pretty amazing. You know that these things are addictive in their habits and you can not break them. To see God come and break the hold of the enemy and set the captives free, that to me is the greatest miracle of all! That's the start of a new life!

"if anyone is in Christ, he is a new creation; old things have passed away; behold, all things have become new" (2 Cor. 5:17 NKJV). Born again, set free from sin. Hallelujah! Glory to God!

God Is God

I found out that God is God in the air, He is God on the land, and He's God in the sea. He is God. Hallelujah! There were many places in Belize that we could not get to by road, so we went by boat. We had a motorcycle to get to some places where other vehicles couldn't go. We had vehicles to get to some places we could get to. We had an airplane to get to places that we could not get to otherwise; and we had places that we couldn't get to with any type of transportation, so we walked. In this particular case; there was a village on an island way out in the Caribbean Sea that the Lord spoke to our hearts about.

At that time we were in a city wide campaign in the second largest city in Belize, called Stann Creek. We had two young men from "Christ for the Nations" that had come down that summer to work with us, and some students that had gone to "Christ for the Nations" from Belize that were working with us, and some other students from Belize. We had a sixty by ninety foot tent set up. We had to have two services a day to accommodate the people. In the afternoon all the children would gather and we would fill that tent up. If we didn't have an afternoon service for them they would take up all the space in the evening service and there would be no room for the adults. So we had an afternoon service with the children and teenagers and ministered to them, and then in the evening we would fill it up with the adults.

We had prayer meeting and sharing time together with all the group of our team every morning. We gathered and prayed and sought God. I have found that we needed to seek for the presence of God to take over because in that whole area there was a lot of witchcraft, voodoo and all that kind of stuff. So you need the presence of God to overcome those evil spirits, because what they do is, they come to try and bind you, and hinder the service. They come to bind the hearts so the people can't hear. So we gathered and prayed every morning for about two or three hours.

Holy Spirit's Leading

One morning in prayer, the Lord began to deal with me to take the tent to this certain island, set it up there and have a revival. I did not want to go there. It's too hard to get there; plus I know the area, and I know that there are a lot of drugs and stuff going on in that village, and I didn't want to go, so I didn't say anything.

In a little while, one of the students spoke up and said, "You know, God is dealing with me that we are supposed to go to this certain village."

"Really?" I asked.

Somebody else spoke up and said, "God has been putting it on my heart that we're supposed to go and have a crusade there."

"Okay Lord, okay; we will do it," I said, *"in the mouth of two or three witnesses, every word shall be established"* (Matt. 18:16; 2 Cor. 13:1).

On this particular Sunday night after we closed the crusade, we split up. Some went back to the city, and some went to this village where we had our 23 foot sailboat. We had just had it all redone and any weak places fixed and painted. It was a 23 foot sailboat with a little 10 horsepower engine on it. It's about 5 miles down the river until you get out to the sea, and you can't sail in the river. We had that little boat but we had this entire big tent, and the boards. The seats were just boards.

We were going to get some cinder blocks in the village, but we needed these boards to put on them so the people would have places to sit. So we had the tent and all these big long 2x12 boards on this boat. It was pretty heavy loaded. Part of the group went back to the city and had a meeting there. Part of us stayed in the village there; and at midnight we all gathered back at the boat. Two of the young men from "Christ for the Nations" and the native brother and myself were going to take the boat and sail it down to this village on an island.

There was a widow woman in the village we were sailing from that had cut quite a few stalks of plantains, that somebody was suppose to come and buy. She was a widow woman and this was her livelihood and they didn't come. So she asked me if I could possibly take these plantains to this village where we were going because they didn't have any there, and I'm sure they would make a quick sale for her. Now, the boat was already heavy loaded, but I just could not tell her, "no," because I knew that was her livelihood. So we put those on board. We were not sitting out of the water very much.

A Sinking Boat Floats

At midnight we had a little moon light so we started down the river. The young native man operating the boat was very experienced. He was raised on the Caribbean Sea, so he knew how to maneuver and operate in the sea. We turned on the little engine and sailed down the river.

These two young men who were sitting up on the boat were saying, "Oh, this is heaven," because in the moonlight sailing down the river through the jungles was gorgeous.

We got out to the sea. Of course in the sea if you're going to sail you've got to have wind. If you don't have any wind you don't go anywhere, but when you have wind you have waves. It's kind of like life, isn't it?

Anyway, we got out to sea for about 30 minutes and something began to feel funny. The boat was no longer sailing; it was just kind of wallowing in the sea. We discovered that there was water coming up from the bottom of this boat somewhere.

So one of the young men from "Christ for the Nations" said, "Well, I'll bail it."

We had to open the hold and get down there and bail it out. You know; he got down there and didn't last but for a few minutes, and he got so seasick he couldn't stand it. So the other young man got in the hole and started bailing; but he also got sick, now there is only one left, and that was me. I do not like close places; claustrophobia you know; and I do not like to go under the water. So I got down and started to bail and I was feeling water way up on my legs, almost to my knee. The whole bottom of this boat was full of water!

You know, Jesus said, "Watch and pray," well, I was bailing and praying.

I was praying, you know; and the young man that was sailing the boat, says, "Brethren, we're going down!"

You could tell that he was scared. So I thought if he was scared, it was time for me to get scared as well. Were we going down way out in the Caribbean Sea, about 1:30 or 2:00 o'clock in the morning? Uh-uh, NO, we don't want to go down! So I was bailing and praying, and all of a sudden it was like Jesus was there with me, but He had to quicken something to me--His Word. His Word has power! There was evidence the boat was going down, the boat was not sailing. Not only was water coming up from the bottom, but now the waves were going over the side of the boat and coming in!

All of a sudden the example that Jesus gave us in Scripture when the boat was about to sink, came to me. Jesus was in the stern of the boat, sleeping; and his disciples came and woke Him up, *"Master, carest thou not that we perish?"* (Mark 4:38), they asked. He told them to go to the other side, didn't He? He did. He got in the boat and told them where to go, and they were going. He was lying down and went to sleep, a storm came up, and they were afraid. Now these were experienced fishermen, but let me tell you something; when a boat you're on is going down in the sea in the night, fear will come on you! If you're alive it will come on you; but God is greater.

When these verses came to me, all of a sudden they became alive in me by the Holy Spirit.

"Do you really think that boat could sink with Jesus on board? Absolutely not! How could that boat sink with Jesus on board?" I thought.

No wonder He said, *"O ye of little faith"* (Matt. 8:26), to them.

Well, all of a sudden, this whole saying came back to me, and I began to talk to the Lord.

"You're just as much on board this boat tonight as you were on that boat that night, because You told us to go to this village. You said, *"You go and lo I will be with you"* (Matt. 28:19-20). We are going at Your command, You are here with us, and this boat can NOT sink!" I said.

That's what I said. You know where fear went? It left, and faith took over! Fear and faith don't mix. Fear will nullify faith but when faith comes in fear has to go. Just like darkness does when you turn on the light, fear left!

This was my declaration and why I am sharing this, because I want us to believe. I want us to believe; *"all things are possible to him that believeth"* (Mark 9:23). Believe, only believe! He is going to do the work.

Our part is simply saying, "God, *'I know whom I have believed'* (2 Tim. 1:12), and I know You are with me!"

So what happened was, I was still bailing, but now I could feel the water going down. The boat was getting lighter and we were starting to sail again! These two men sitting up there on the boat were so sick.

"Ooooh, Brother, how much longer?" they asked the young man sailing the boat.

When he said it would be about another two hours, "Oh no," they said, "My goodness, another two hours?"

You see, all that fun they had when we started turned the other way now. This is the way life is sometimes, that's why we don't go by feelings, we go by faith. I've found that going by faith means that you go on anyway, no matter how you feel. You trust God anyway. No matter what the circumstances are, you go on anyway.

The boat began to rise up and we began to sail. Just after daylight we sailed into this village, pulled up by the shore, and began to unload our boat. We had to carry our cargo a ways through the water. We carried all these plantain, the big tent; all the boards and everything, and unloaded it. Just as we were getting unloaded, the "boat right man" came. They called him "inches," because he was very tall, and he was the fellow in this fishing village that repaired the boats when they needed repairing.

So I told him, "Inches, take this boat around to your shop and work on it, because there is something bad wrong with this boat. There's a hole somewhere in the bottom of this boat; but God brought us in here. If it hadn't have been for God we would be at the bottom of the Caribbean Sea."

"Okay, Brother Hooper, okay, okay," he replied.

He took the boat to his place to work on it. There was no road in this sandy village just a sidewalk.

It wasn't very long until he came back down that sidewalk through the village telling everybody, "Well, Brother Hooper said God brought them in here. I want to tell you that's for sure, because that boat could not sail with the size of hole it has in the bottom of it!"

Now let me tell you, God's Word has power; when we believe it! Why am I saying this? I'm telling you this to encourage your faith; the same reason that God put all the testimonies in His Word. Didn't He put them in there for us? He said He did.

He said, *"They are written for our admonition, upon whom the ends of the world are come."* (1 Cor. 10:11).

That must mean us! God had these things written down in His Book to the intent we would believe. Praise God! Hallelujah!

Results of Faithfulness

We were driving into this same village where we kept the sailboat some years before, and I had been in there many times. It was very, very difficult to get into this village because the road was so bad and the mud and everything, made it just horrible to get there. I had gone in and out of this village many times with these big speakers and set up the microphone, and just shared Jesus with these people. I wouldn't see anybody and didn't know what was going on.

Finally this one particular time I was going, and said, "God, if I don't see something, some results somewhere this time; I don't think I'm going to come back in here again."

But as I drove in the village I met some men coming up to my truck.

"Preacher, we've been listening to you all these times you've come in here, and we've decided that the next time you come, we want to get the community center and have a big service; and just see what all you've got to say," they said.

My heart just leaped inside of me. You know, sometimes we feel like giving up just about the time the victory is on the way. About the time God is doing what we don't know He's doing, so we just feel like; well, it's just too hard. No, it's not. What I'm saying is, feelings sometimes play tricks on us; but God is faithful anyway.

"Yes sir, that would be just fine," I replied.

Have you ever wondered what the Lord wanted you to say? What subject He wanted you to preach? Absolutely. I believe God has a right Word, for the right people, at the right time and place.

"God," I asked, "what do you want me to share tonight?"

I was excited, and the Lord spoke to my heart.

"I want you to preach on healing," He answered.

I said, "Wait a minute, Lord, these people are afraid of anything that has to do with the 'supernatural,' anything that's not ordinary. They're very superstitous and scared. You mean you want me to run them all off after they got here now?"

You know what? It didn't change His mind one bit.

He said, "I want you to preach on healing."

"But God, these people need salvation," I said.

"Preach on healing," He repeated.

You know, it's amazing how we think our way is better, and that our plans are better. It seemed to me like what the Lord would do, would be to save them and then heal them, but He reversed it on me.

Did you know that the Scripture says, *"the goodness of God leadeth thee [people] to repentance?"* (Rom. 2:4).

God had a plan. All He wanted me to do was to be obedient to what He wanted to do.

So I said, "Okay Lord, we'll do that."

So everybody came to the Community Center and packed it out. The building was pretty big and there were steps going up on both sides. The building was packed and all the steps going up each side was packed. I opened my Bible and began to read the Scriptures about the stripes that were laid upon Jesus for our healing. I shared for about 15 minutes on divine healing, and God's purpose for our healing.

Then I made this statement, "Anybody here that wants to be healed, come forward."

To my surprise nobody left.

"Thank You, Jesus," I said.

I'm not knocking the way anybody else does, but the way the Lord directed me to do this was to say, anybody that wants to be healed, not prayed for; *healed*, come forward.

Jesus Healed All

Well, to my amazement people began to get up and come. They lined up the whole way across the front of the building. Did you know that every single person that came was healed? Every single one of them!

When we got to the end of that line, there was an older man standing there.

"Brother, my wife is in Belize City in the hospital, and she is supposed to be operated on in the morning. Do you think that God could hear your prayer here, and heal her over there?" he inquired.

Belize City was several miles from where we were.

"Absolutely!" I said.

So we laid hands on him and spoke healing to his wife in the hospital in Belize City. She never had to have the operation, and lived for many, many years after that. I remember when we laid hands on this older gentleman to pray for his wife, he began to shake. What was that? It was the presence and the power of God! He had never ever felt that before in his whole life. Thus began a mighty work of God in that village.

After they all were healed, I told them they could go back and sit down. Then I preached on the mercy of the Lord and the goodness of God to forgive us. He not only heals all our diseases, but He forgives all our iniquities; all of them. All our diseases, all our iniquities, there is no difference between. What sin is there that God would not forgive? We know about the blaspheming of the Holy Ghost, I'm not talking about that, but I'm asking; what sin have we committed that He will not forgive us of? Don't we believe when we ask Him that He does forgive us? Well then, what sickness is there that He can't heal us of? So when we believe for Him to heal us, then we believe it just like for our Salvation.

Here is my confession; "I am healed because God's Word says I am!"

The stripes that were placed upon His body were for my healing; that's for me. So I am healed, I was healed; and I'm being healed. I am saved, I was saved; and I'm being saved. Praise God! We must make positive confessions according to the Word of God, or the enemy will steal it. He will try and steal it, but he can't have it when you believe God's Word. You don't have to go to his camp and take it back, because he couldn't get it in the first place. It's better to hold onto it, instead of letting him have it, then go try and get it back. We are going to hold on to what God said, the Holy Spirit inspired Gospel.

Holy Ghost Revival

So God began a tremendous work in that village and He began to pour out His Spirit. We built a tabernacle there with a dirt floor. We put up some big beams and a metal roof, but the sides were all open, so the people walking up and down the little pathway along the river would hear and see and know what God was doing. We weren't trying to fence God in or fence anybody out, so we just had a tabernacle. God began to move in such a way, people were being "slain in the Spirit." By that I mean the Spirit of God would move on them and they'd find themselves in the dirt. Not on the carpet, not somebody catching them, but there in the dirt, and when they came up, they would come up speaking in tongues. What is that? That's God's presence honoring His Word.

I remember one lady, she was probably about 7 or 8 months expecting, and she got up out of her seat, about halfway back, and started toward the front. All of a sudden the Holy Ghost hit her and, wham, right on her back and, bam, she hit the ground.

Somebody said, "That couldn't be God, you know, just lay this expectant mother down like that, it couldn't be God."

I said, "It was. Who else did it? Nobody touched her."

She got up, and started toward the front again; and wham, down she went.

So the next day I asked her, "Sister, let me ask you a question, what happened to you when you hit the ground?"

"Brother, I don't know, but I had been having all kinds of problems and back trouble, and everything else, and I haven't had any since," she answered.

I'm telling you, this thing that we're talking about is for real— it's for real. Praise God! And it's for real for all of us; but we say, *"Lord, I believe; help thou mine unbelief"* (Mark 9:24).

We need to pray, "Lord, help me to believe everything you said, not just part of it, but everything; to absolutely believe."

Jesus said, *"Whatever you ask if you don't doubt in your heart, it'll be done."* (See, Mark 11:23-24).

Doubt Not in Your Heart

The enemy is a genus at putting thoughts in our minds. The battleground is in our minds.

He knows what thoughts to put in your mind, and then comes back around and says, "Uh-huh, you're not going to get it because you didn't believe."

He has stolen many things from me in the past with that trick. He came to Jesus in the wilderness and said, *"If thou be the son of God"* (Matt. 4:3).

Now, he didn't come to him in a form like a human form, I'm sure, because the Bible says that Jesus was tempted in all points just the same way we are.

So I believe that Satan came to Jesus in His mind. *"If You are the Son of God,"* (Matt. 4:6 NKJV).

What was he doing? He was trying to make Him doubt.

Now, I'll put my little version in here. After 40 days in the wilderness with no baths, no shave, no food, no water, this is what Satan wants to do is cause us to look at circumstances; how you feel, how you look, and all these kinds of things.

He says, "You don't look like the Son of God. Look at you, you're a mess. You stink, you're ugly, and you're hungry. If you were the Son of God, you wouldn't be in this condition."

Does the devil ever come around your house and say, "If you are really a child of God, you wouldn't be going through this test or that test?"

He's a genus at putting doubt in your mind, and then come back around and say, "See there now, you doubted, so you're not going to get what you asked God for."

But Jesus said, *"and shall not doubt in his heart"* (Mark 11:23).

There is a difference, because Satan can put doubts and thoughts in your mind, but not everything that comes to your mind is in your heart. So that's why we need this settled in our hearts, we need God's Word as an anchor; settled in our heart. So when the enemy comes, we don't argue with him, we just give him back the Word; just like Jesus did. Give him back what the Bible says; because he can not contend with the Word of God, he has to back off. Jesus was subject to the temptation of the enemy, and so are we. As long as we are in this flesh, we will be subject to the fiery darts, the trials and the tests that the enemy wants to bring against us. But if we will believe the Word of God, we will come out on the winning side and have a brand new testimony, and the purpose of the enemy will be defeated!

When Jesus was crucified and gave up the ghost, they took his body and buried Him.

Then He went into hell itself to pay the penalty for our sin.

The devil laughed, "Oh, I've got Him now; I've got Him now."

He rejoiced because he had turned the people against Him and caused them to cry out, "Crucify Him; crucify Him."

"I've got Him now, He's in hell; He will never get out of here!"

But on that third day when Jesus arose and took the keys of hell and of death; the devil said, "I wish I would have left Him alone. Now look what I've done, I've opened the door for eternal salvation to who ever believes."

It was his own undoing to crucify Jesus. Now I believe that comes right on down to you and me.

No matter what he does, no matter how he comes against us, if we will stand on the Word, we will see God work and the devil will say, "I wish I would have left them alone."

Because all he does, is just gives us a brand new testimony. Don't you like testimonies? Yeah, I do, but I don't like the test. I never have come to like them yet.

I remember reading a testimony by Brother C. T. Studd. Many

years ago, back in the 1800's, he was one of the first missionaries to go into Africa.

He went through a whole lot of things, and he made this statement, "You know, I got to where I just enjoyed getting into situations just to see how God was going to get me out."

"God, I'm not there yet," I said.

I'm not there yet, are you? To me, that's the top rung of the ladder. Now, that's not creating situations, but I'm telling you, he was in Cannibal country; head hunting country. He did get in the boiling pot, and God got him out.

But he said, "It's so exciting."

If you're going into a test, no matter what that test may be, you can go into it as a new adventure in God, it's a new step, it is a new testimony. You know God's not going to fail you; you know you have the victory, because He gave it to us.

He conquered the enemy and gave us the victory over the enemy. *"Behold, I give you power to tread on serpents and scorpions, and over ALL the power of the enemy; and nothing shall by any means hurt you."* (Luke 10:19)

Isn't that what He said? Not just some, but all the power of the enemy, so we know we have the victory. We know we are going to win.

We can praise God in the middle of a test and say, "I'm right now in the middle of a brand new testimony."

So whether it's in the air in an airplane, in the sea in a boat, or on the highway, we can trust God to bring us through. Praise God!

Angels Help

We were going through Mexico. We did this many times. On this one occasion, my cousin was driving a 15 passenger van. It was to be used in the mission work in Belize. Our daughter was driving a pickup truck behind me.

We have navigated through Mexico at different times with as many as ten vehicles in a caravan. The two driving behind me didn't know the way, so I was leading them through Mexico. There was only three in this caravan.

Of course with radios, cell phones and all that, you could stay in contact, but in those days we didn't have any of those. When I would go around a car and maybe it was on a hill or a curve, if there was nobody coming when I got up there and saw that there was nobody coming, I would put on the left blinker. When I put that on they would know it was safe to come around.

Some people get real scared and say, "What are you doing going around?"

Well, because the leader up there says it's safe. Now there are many curves in our life, and we don't know what is what, but there is One that's looking out for us.

He is our leader and He says, "I am with you, It's safe, come on around."

I passed this eighteen-wheeler, and our daughter came around behind me, but I saw a little black pickup truck really coming fast, and I did not give a signal for the other van to go around. My cousin, who was driving the other van; pulled out to go around this truck, with the pickup he couldn't see, coming very fast at them. Two of our daughters were in that van along with him. I knew something had to happen because he did not have space to get back in. He did not have enough time to make it around that truck! The roads were narrow, with a big embankment on the side.

I cried, "Jesus!"

I was watching him in the mirror and all of a sudden--whoosh, down that embankment they went. The pickup went on. I never even saw his brake lights come on and he didn't even slow down. There are some crazy drivers in Mexico. As soon as I could get over, I pulled over. Our daughter driving the pickup pulled over behind me, and we made a U-turn to go back.

She couldn't figure out what was going on, and I just said, "The van!"

We took off to go back. We got back there and somebody had cleared off a small space, probably to plant corn or something; I don't know, but it was cleared off; and that's exactly where that van went, down that very steep embankment. A fifteen passenger van is very top heavy, but that thing went bouncing over the edge, and down in there, and never turned over! We had a big ice chest in the back with things in it. The ice chest flew over both seats, and stuff flew out and hit one of our daughters in the head, but they were okay. When I came back around the corner, I saw our van sitting there at an angle, but it hadn't even turned over.

I said, "Thank you Jesus; thank you Jesus!"

I was also driving a fifteen passenger van. So I parked it and went running down there.

My cousin said, "I'm sorry for treating your van like this."

"I'm not concerned about the van, I'm concerned about you and the children, about all of you inside this van," I said.

Because by the law of gravity and everything else, it should have been just rolling over and over down that hill, but it never turned over!

He said, "I hit something. When it stopped, it stopped like I hit something."

I went out in front of the van and looked. There wasn't anything there, except, it was about to go over into this pool of water, this slue thing of water down in there. If it would have gone a little bit further and the wheels ran in that, it would have dumped it over into this big pool of water.

"No, the angels are with you, they are riding in this van. They kept it from turning over and then they stopped it before it went too far!" I said.

Just about that time, a pickup loaded with police, there must have been about ten or fifteen policemen in the back of this truck; pulled up there and stopped. Now in Mexico, if you have any kind of accident; you run off the road, or whatever, they throw the book at you. So they got out of the truck, all of them and came down there. This guy got his book out, and he was writing us up.

I'm telling you; the Spirit of the Lord came on my wife and she went right over there, got right in his face, and told him off! I mean, she told him off. The man closed his book, turned around like a dog with his tail between his legs, and walked right back up that bank and they got in their truck! Now, I don't know if that man understood English, or not; but if he didn't God was interpreting for him. I've seen that happen several times in Mexico; but it's not her, it's the Lord. She didn't tell him in a bad way, she just told him the truth; and he just walked off, and they sat up there in their truck and watched us.

Down the road just a little ways was a dump truck. I walked down there to see if the driver would come and pull us back up, because it was almost straight up getting out of there. He was going to do it until these policemen came, because it is against the law to help anybody in Mexico. Now that's a crazy law, isn't it? That must be the devil's law.

So now he wouldn't do it, but he loaned us his chain, a big long log chain. I turned my van around, and had a tow strap and hooked onto this chain, and stayed up on the road and hooked it onto the van.

I told my cousin, "Don't try to move it until I start to move."

My wife and the girls were hanging on the side of the van where the doors open to counter balance the van and keep it from turning over. When we got all ready I put it in gear, and it went uuurrumph. Now those police knew there wasn't any way we were going to pull that van out of there, with this other van on the road, and they weren't offering to help us either.

So I got out and walked back down, and asked my cousin, "Are you sure you've got it in drive?"

He had it in park, and it wasn't going anywhere that way.

"Put it in drive, and when you feel me tighten up on the chain, just give it a little bit of gas," I said.

I got in and started pulling with the van I was driving, and this time it went on up and towed that van right up on the road!

Those guys couldn't believe what they were seeing. Not only did the angels keep it from turning over, but I believe they got behind it and helped push it on up the hill!

The Bible says, *"The angel of the Lord encamps all around those who fear Him, and delivers them"* (Ps. 34:7 NKJV).

They are encamped about us, and I believe they helped push us and get us up the hill, and out on the road. Hallelujah!

So I stopped, unhooked the other van and took the tow chain back to the driver of the dump truck.

I said to the others in our caravan, "The road is so narrow, we're going to drive down the road, and as soon as we find a place wide enough for all of us to get off, we'll pull off and check the van and see what damage there was, if any, and see what happened to it."

So we got to a place where we could pull over, and all the police went by and honked and waved at us. We checked the van and not even a hubcap was missing, nothing!

I'm telling you, God is *"a very present help in* (every time of) *trouble"* (Ps. 46:1). "He is always there, and when it's His angels that's the same as if He were there." *"He gives His angels charge over us to keep us"* (See, Ps. 91:11).

They are always watching over us, to keep us. It would be nice if they kept us from all the tests and trials. They don't do that, but they help us through them. They play their part, but we've got to play our part; and that is to believe.

The Shrunken Cars

On another occasion I was pulling a van behind my van, my wife and family and another sister from Alabama was with us. My wife and the children were laying in the van asleep, and this sister was sitting in the front seat with me. We were talking and sharing things of the Lord and everything, and came around a curve. There was a big embankment on both sides of the road, and there was a car parked dead still in my lane! This guy was standing out behind his car trying to wave me down, but coming into this curve, I didn't see him until I was pretty close to him. Then I was aware that there was another car coming from the other direction! We were going to meet right where that stalled car was. Now, what do you do in a case like that? I couldn't stop because the van in tow behind me is pushing me, and besides; you have to be real careful when you've got a vehicle on a tow bar back there, it'll start fishtailing on you and turn you over. So, I applied the brakes as much as I could, but I knew I couldn't stop. If I didn't stop and ran into the back of that car, it would definitely kill that man standing there.

So again, I just cried, "Jesus!"

All of a sudden--whoosh--it just felt like everything shrank; everything just shrank!

I came so close to that car and the other car coming, there was no way we were going to pass on that one lane! One of us was going to hit that car or the other was going off of the embankment, but we *both* went right through there. He went on, and we went right through. It just felt like something had shrunk us.

So when we got through, I asked this sister, "Did you feel that?"

She said, "I sure did; God shrunk us, He just shrunk us! He just put the pressure on, and shrunk us so we could get in through that little bitty narrow spot!"

We never touched the other car, never touched the car that went through, and he never went off the side of the embankment. I want to tell you, *"God is a present help in our time of need"* (See, Ps. 46:1). He is there.

Not too long after we had gotten to Belize, we had an old Jeep Wagoneer we went down there in, and my dad was there. It was his first trip down to Belize, with all the family. We had about ten people or so in that Jeep Wagoneer.

We were going down south to some of the villages and came to a real narrow spot in the road. All of the bridges are one lane and this narrow spot was right before a bridge. Below us was a big cit-rus grove, and from the road we where looking down on the tops of the trees. Here came a Land Rover, coming around a curve, to meet us through that one lane bridge; just flying. There was not enough space there for two cars to pass!

I said, "I am *not* going to hit this man head-on."

So I pulled over on the side with no shoulder at all on an em-bankment way above the citrus grove. Only two wheels were still on the road. The car never ran off the road and never turned over!

The Lord held that side of the vehicle up while the other vehicle went by us on the other side. I'm telling you; when we got back on the road, we stopped, and we all got out and praised God!

He is our God. He is our Father. He is our sufficiency, and He is our All in All. The Lord wants us just to believe, that is all He requires of us. If you search the Scripture there are many times it talks about believing. I believe we are going to see great things in this generation. God is raising up a multitude of people around the world who believe Him and His Word.

Chapter 6

God Rewards Faithfulness

Bad News Turned Good

While we were there in Oklahoma working on our airplane that had been ground looped, we had just gotten our big school bus loaded and ready to go back to Belize and in it was a tool that we really needed in Belize. It was a big 18,000 kilowatt Onan generator. We lived for months and months and years without any electricity. Can you imagine what it would be like here if all of a sudden you had no more electricity? The Lord provided, and we had that in the bus and a lot of things for the mission work in Belize. A young lady, one of our cousins, had been traveling with us to different churches; and it was time for her to go home when our airplane got wrecked and we couldn't make the journey. So I told our son to take our cousin in the bus and deliver her back home down below San Antonio; and when we got the airplane ready to go, we'd come by, pick up the bus and take it on to Belize.

While we were working on the airplane, I got a call from our son, and he said, "Daddy, I really don't want to tell you this, but the bus threw a rod right through the engine, in Rockwall, Texas."

That is right there close to Dallas.

I immediately said, "Well now Lord, here's another brand new testimony in the making." Then I asked him, "Is there anywhere you could put the bus until we can get an opportunity to come?"

"Well, there's a big beautiful boat company right across the freeway from where I am. I went over and talked to the owner. He said they would bring something and tow it over to their lot and we could park it behind his chain link fence until you have an opportunity to get here," he answered.

"Fine, that'll work, just park it there and go get the greyhound bus or some way and take our cousin home. Make sure she gets home. That's my number one priority right now; that she gets home safely," I said.

So they came and towed the bus over there, and parked it behind their chain link fence. The boat sales owner, decided he would take them to Dallas to the bus station. So he took them all the way from Rockwall to Dallas to the bus station and sent them on their way.

Now when we got through with the plane and everything, we went down to Rockwall. It's not ever exciting to have to roll up your sleeves, get in the grease and get dirty and filthy. There are many times when in the flesh, you don't feel like praising the Lord; but the Scripture says, *"In everything give thanks"* (1 Thess. 5:18).

Does it really mean that; in everything?

You know, there are times when I think, "Even in this Lord, you want me to give thanks in this?"

Do you know why He told us to do that? He told us that because our victory is in our praise and our thanksgiving; that's where our victory is. Our power is in prayer, but our victory is in praise.

He said, "Give thanks."

So I just started giving thanks.

We got there and met the boat sales owner and he was glad to meet us. I was sure hoping to get this thing out of his way pretty soon because it was an ugly looking bus and he had some of the most beautiful expensive boats out at their dealership. He had a big showroom where some of the boats were on display inside.

He said, "Just bring that bus in here and take the engine out."

"No, no, Sir, this bus is so ugly, dirty and greasy, just let us work on it outside here beside the building," I said, then asked, "Have you got a cherry picker?"

"Yes, I've got one of those you can use," he replied.

That's the thing you use to reach in there and lift the engine out when you get it all loose.

So we were out there working, my dad, I, and this same young man that was in the boat with us when it was sinking in the sea. We three were out there working; getting all the bolts out and everything, and he would come out there and just watch us.

"You know, I've never seen preachers that would get greasy," he remarked.

"Well, we're not just preachers, we're missionaries. Missionaries have to do just about anything and everything," I said.

We were used to doing that. We weren't trying to impress him; we were just doing what had to be done.

Finally he asked, "Uh, do you fellows like fish?"

"Well yeah, sure, we like fish," was our answer.

"I'm going to order some fish, and when it gets here, you come in the office and we'll have lunch," he said.

So he got the fish and invited us into his office. I could have had all kinds of bad feelings and everything else, with the bus throwing the rod and the plane getting wrecked, but there was something inside my heart that was rejoicing. It was rejoicing just to see how God was going to work all of these things out.

We just got through fixing the plane, and didn't have a whole lot of money, and now we were going to have to buy an engine for this bus. I didn't know how that was going to work out either, but there was something inside that was causing my heart to rejoice. He is alive. Jesus is always on the scene and no matter what the situation is; He is there.

So when we went in to eat the fish around this big fancy desk in his office, he said, "Preacher, would you like to bless this food?"

I'm telling you, the Holy Ghost came down, and I couldn't stop, it was just pouring out.

I overheard him tell his partner later on, "If you're hungry, don't ask these missionaries to pray."

Anyway, we ate the fish, and he said, "Come in here with me."

We went into another office and he told me, "You know, the Lord put it on my heart to buy you a brand new engine."

How about that!

He said, "It's already on the way over here. It is all paid for and everything, and when you get the heads off, I've already made arrangements with this company right here in Rockwall to do a valve job on both heads, and they will both be new!"

Now, I didn't know God was going to do all of that, but there was something inside that just let me know; "I'm up to this."

I am more than a conqueror, and He is more than enough! Hallelujah!

So we just had a wonderful time, and in a little bit, he came back out there and started asking questions. He was a good Baptist man, he had heard something about the Holy Ghost, and he wanted to know more about this Holy Ghost, and it was hard to get any work done. It's hard to work on greasy cars and share the Word at the same time. Every spare moment he was right there asking questions. He is so hungry for the Holy Spirit.

Then I knew why the bus broke down. The airplane got wrecked so this man and his wife could be saved, and their home could be spared. The bus broke down for this man's hunger for the power of the Holy Spirit in his life! God is a wonderful, good God all the time. So we just had a wonderful time sharing and working, and got the bus all running, and made it back down to Belize.

Transportation Provided

We had to take our children several miles there in Belize to go to school, so I thought, some kind of a used Toyota car would be just the thing. I'm not putting a plug in for Toyota, but we found out that they hold up better than any other vehicle on those rough roads in Belize. The boat sales owner was also a Toyota dealer in Dallas. He had this boat venture in Rockwall, which didn't last too long. He gave that up and became a Toyota dealer.

So I called him up one day, and asked, "Brother, would you happen to have maybe an older Toyota, but still in pretty good shape, that I could buy and bring to Belize?"

So the duty wouldn't be so high, and I'd have a cheaper way. When gas is $12.00 a gallon, you're looking for a cheaper way.

He answered, "Yeah I do, just tell me when you're going to be at the airport and I'll pick you up."

I told him when I would be there and he picked me up at the airport and we went to his place of business.

When we got together it was hard to talk about business because he wanted to talk about the Lord; just hungry. Don't you like people that are hungry for the Lord, and just can't get enough?

"I've got a car here, it's got a little noise in the differential, I don't know exactly what it is, take it out and try it," he said.

So I took it down the road a little ways and came back and I just didn't feel right, because it's a long way from Texas to Belize. It would have a long journey ahead of it and then when you get there you need something that is going to give you some service. So I took it for a short drive and came back.

"Well, how did you like it?" he asked.

I was just being honest and said, "I didn't."

I really didn't. I don't think you should put on airs, just say what you mean and mean what you say.

"Well, I'm sure glad you don't because I've got one picked out for you," he said.

It was a brand new Toyota station wagon sitting out there waiting to be serviced!

"I want you to take that one," he said.

I said, "Oh no, brother, I couldn't do that."

"Look, I'm giving it to Jesus. You got anything to say to that?" he said.

What could I say to that?

He said, "God has been so good to me, I just want to do something for Him and I'm going to give Him this brand new car!" Then he told his service people, "Take it in there run it at the head of the line, service it out, and get it ready to go!"

So they got it all ready to go. He had them put an extra spare tire in it and some extra spare parts and things. He also had them take it down and fill it up with gas!

Then he said, "Now, you're ready to go."

Could you believe that? Who would have ever believed that a bus breaking down in front of his boat place would ever work out like that? It's God's provision! I don't believe that we should go around begging. I see a lot of preachers doing that. I don't believe in doing that. I believe in the One that called me, the One that's able to supply, and the One that's able to do what He said He would do! Hallelujah!

God has proven it over and over and over. I believe these are the things the Lord wants people to know, *"that I am well able"* (Rom. 4:21).

We were friends for a long time, and after a couple of years he called me and said, "Brother Hooper, that car is probably about worn out. I want you to bring it back up here, I've got another brand new one to take its place."

Isn't that something?

No wonder Paul, under the inspiration of the Holy Spirit said, *"In everything give thanks; for this is the will of God in Christ Jesus concerning you"* (1 Thess. 5:18).

God Inhabits Praise

I remember reading about two men in the Bible that were thrown in prison. Shamed and beaten, with their backs bleeding, their hands and feet fastened in the stocks in the inner chamber; where they put the worst criminals.

The Bible said, *"they began to sing and to praise the Lord"* (Acts 16:25). There wasn't anybody to encourage them, there wasn't any music around, but they just began singing and making melody in their hearts to the Lord.

At the same time there was worshiping going on in heaven, but the Lord heard their singing above it all.

It so blessed the Lord that He said, "Hush, wait just a minute, I hear something coming from a jailhouse. Listen to that; listen to that! Go down there and shake that place up, turn them loose, show them that I'm alive!" Hallelujah!

So the angel came, shook the whole place up, turned all the prisoners loose, not just Paul and Silas; and the Bible said that's where revival actually started in Macedonia.

Is He the same today? Can He do that today? Yes He can! We've got doors that you can just walk up to now, and they just, whoosh, open up and let you go through. They didn't have them back in Peter's day, but God had one! It didn't have an electric eye, it had the *"all seeing eye"* on it and when he walked up to that gate, it just opened of its own accord, and Peter went right on through. God wants us to know that what He has ever done He can still do! Hallelujah, praise God!

A Higher Authority

We had helped in a big city crusade in Belize City, the largest city in Belize. Not real big compared to a lot of our big cities, but it is the biggest city in Belize. The Lord laid it on this brother's heart from Mexico, to bring a huge tent, and set it up in Belize City. We knew him and had visited his mission in Mexico before, so he came to our house and we went to Belize City to see about setting this big tent up.

"You can't set that tent up in Belize City anywhere," the authorities said, "You can't do it."

So I looked at this gentleman and said, "Well Sir, I'm just going to have to go over your head."

He looked at me with a scowl on his face like, "You think you're defying me?"

I just made a plain statement, "I'm going over your head;" because this brother said the Lord put it on his heart to come to this city, and set up this tent and have a crusade.

So we left that place, had a prayer meeting, and went over his head. While we were praying the Lord laid some fellows on my heart to go talk to.

I went and talked to them, and they said, "Yes sir, you can sure have a place out there on the beach. Right there in the city but on the beach on the Caribbean Sea. You can have that place."

We took the tent he brought out there and set it up, and set up our tent right by it, and it was the prayer tent. We printed a whole bunch of leaflets, and different ones of the team started going through the city handing them out.

"Make sure you take some pamphlets to that office that said we couldn't set the tent up." I said.

While we were in the plane flying over the different villages dropping out leaflets; some of the others were passing through the city handing them out. Those who were passing out leaflets in the city said when they gave out those pamphlets in that office, the people who worked there could hardly believe what they were looking at. But God moved in a marvelous way. Many people gave their hearts to the Lord in that crusade. I wasn't the preacher for that crusade, I was the helper. I was in charge of the first part of the meeting and led the singing and all that. At the end of that crusade we had to leave for the States.

Broken Truck Healed

We had some people from the states with us and some students going to "Christ for the Nations" in Dallas, that needed to get to the U.S. We left that meeting that night and started for the U.S. in a 1974 Ford super cab pickup with fourteen people on board. We had three in the front, four in the back seat, and seven in a camper with a bed and all of our luggage; so we were loaded. We left Belize City after service that night to drive straight through to the U.S. After we had traveled several miles in Mexico and was way out in one of the most desolate parts of that country, I looked in the mirror and all I could see was a black cloud of smoke coming out from under the truck. It was like I was leaving a smoke screen! Instantly my heart leaped within me; something was bad wrong.

I pulled over to the side of the road. As far as I could see back down the road, was a stream of transmission fluid. I knew instantly what had happened. The torque converter seal broke in that truck and poured all the transmission fluid out. When I stopped, in just a jiffy there was a huge puddle underneath the truck.

I shut the truck off, and prayed, "I don't know Lord what to do?"

I do know one thing. Either the engine or the transmission has to come out to replace that torque converter seal. I don't speak Spanish and we were miles from nowhere, and I have fourteen people that

I'm responsible for! Sometimes the trials the Lord lets us go through are not always pretty; they're not always convenient and they are not something that we would choose.

By now the sun was shining very hot, so I walked around in the shade of that truck, squatted down and put my head down to talk to the Lord.

One of the students that I had been sharing Jesus with, said to me, "Why don't we pray."

I thought, yes, there isn't anything better we could do. Let's just pray; yeah that's a good idea. So we began to pray. Now, as I told you, prayer is power, so we began to pray. When we began to pray, God began to work!

God began to lift us out of that place of helplessness and hopelessness, and what do we do now, into a place of believing Him. So we got up from our prayer meeting, and all fourteen of us laid hands on that truck, and ask God to heal it. When we got through praying, I turned on the key and the engine started! I looked underneath the truck and there wasn't anything coming out.

"I guess all the fluid is gone," I said.

You always check your transmission with the engine idling, so I left it idling and kept looking, and there wasn't anything coming out at all. I raised up the hood, pulled out the dip stick, wiped it off, pushed it back in, pulled it out again, and it read full! Talk about a rejoicing and shouting good time on the side of the road! Hallelujah!

I drove that truck all the way to the states, all over the states and back to Belize. Until the day I sold it I never put another drop of transmission fluid in it! Now, if you're mechanically minded at all it would be a little hard for you to believe that, wouldn't it?

But our God is *"a very present help in every time of trouble"* (Ps. 46:1).

I just love Him, don't you? He just wants to magnify Himself in us.

When we first went to Belize we went in an old Jeep Wagoneer. It took us fourteen days from the border of Texas to Belize, and we slept in the car. Fourteen days! All the bridges that are toll bridges now were ferries then. Sometimes it would take you all day long just to get across on one ferry. The mud would be so bad it would be hard to go. Many times I was sure glad for that four wheel drive, but it was very difficult. I'm not really a fan of the Jeep Wagoneer. In less than a year; Belize shook that vehicle all to pieces.

Cheerful Givers

We had a little Honda 90 trail bike. They are designed to take a person out into the woods hunting and when you kill a deer you can strap it on the back. It has four speeds over and four speeds under. It will climb a hill and almost fall backwards on you. It doesn't go really fast, but it will get there. Another brother and I went to Belize City on this trail bike. Because there were no roads to get to the southern part, everything was done by boat. We took our little Honda motorcycle aboard the passenger & freight ship and went south. It was only about 100 miles, but it took us 24 hours to get there! We unloaded our bike off of the boat, and started to find our way around. Since it was our first time there we had to stop and ask people how to get to each village. Sometimes it was just a trail leading from one village to another. Anytime we would meet anyone, we would stop and talk to them about Jesus. We went into those villages and just took Jesus. It was like talking a foreign language. We are so blessed, aren't we?

We went to village after village, even without a road. We made it through 105 miles of jungle before we reached back to civilization. I remember crossing some of those low-water bridges that had 8-inch planks with spaces in between them. It was a struggle trying to ride our motorcycle across those planks with two people. The man on the back was wiggling around, trying to look this way and that, and when he did; the wheel would drop down into one of those cracks.

We got stuck many times. So after the first bridge I told him that he would need to walk across. These are some experiences that are really not funny at the time. Then you have to deal with sand flies, mosquitoes, doctor flies, snakes, and all kinds of wild animals.

We finally made it back to a town and there was an Assembly of God church there. We were so happy to go in and sit down in this church, and receive a little bit. When you're giving out all the time, it's nice just to be able to receive. So we sat down, and after the service, the missionary came and we got acquainted with him.

"I want you to go home with me," he said.

We accepted his gracious invitation. He lived up in the valley which is a very beautiful citrus grove in Belize. We had a really good time with him, staying up until late into the night. He invited us to come back, so we went and preached for him; just sharing Jesus.

This burden for the lost just would not go away, but I knew I couldn't get there very well on this trail bike. There was a couple that came down from Missouri to visit us in Belize. At that time I began to feel a drawing to the southern part of the country where there were hardly any roads at all. When they saw what was happening and what the Lord was doing, they wanted to do something.

"What you need is a Jeep, a four-wheel drive Jeep, to get to where you need to go. When I get back home, I'm going to find one and we're going to get you a Jeep," he said.

I thought that would be a good idea, because I wanted to get there, I didn't care how I got there; but I wanted to get there with the Gospel.

I never have just stopped to count how many churches the Lord Himself started in our ministry in Belize, but it was a whole lot. Now up here in the Untied States they call it planting churches but there is no planting there, there's nothing there, it's pioneering. You don't go and sleep in motels, and eat in the fancy restaurants. There are none there, and that's pioneering.

So this minister and his wife came home. He was out having a revival meeting and there were some young fellows that had their own band that got saved in his revival.

He had said something about needing a Jeep for Belize, and they said, "We've got one we don't need anymore 'cause we're not going to play in that band anymore, you can have ours."

So he called me, and said, "Brother Samuel, we've got the Jeep, and we'll pay your ticket to come get it!" Well, praise God!

I said, "Alright."

So we flew up to Missouri and got there late in the evening. The next morning we were sitting around the table eating breakfast, and I notice this minister friend wasn't looking real happy. He was deep in thought about something.

Finally he said, "You know, I don't really think that Jeep is what you need in Belize. What you need is a four-wheel drive Ford pick-up with a camper, so when you get to those villages you will have a place to lie down, rest and sleep if you need to."

"I'm going to go, I'll be back in a little while," he said.

So he left.

Let me tell you something, *"God loves a cheerful giver"* (2 Cor. 9:7), and God will bless a cheerful giver.

He called the Elders of his church together and said, "You know, we are never afraid to go and buy stuff for ourselves on the credit. I know we don't have the money right here but don't you think we could take a step of faith and on the credit, buy Brother Samuel a brand new four-wheel drive Ford pickup?"

Now, I don't know what's going on, I don't know any of that. They all agreed! So he came back, and now he was all smiles.

"Well Brother Samuel, we've decided that we would just trade that Jeep in on this brand new Ford four-wheel drive pick-up truck!" he tells me.

It was red. You know, I was happy, and at the same time I was sad.

"Let me pray about this," I replied.

I went upstairs, and got down before the Lord, and said, "God, the people that I minister to are poor, poor people. If in any way this brand new vehicle is going to make them feel like I think I'm better than they are; I don't want it. I know the intentions are good, but if it's going to hinder what You want to do with these people, I'd rather crawl to get there."

Because the value of souls was heavy on my heart, that's why I was there. I was not there to show off beautiful equipment, I was there to reach them for Jesus.

"God, I don't want anything to hinder what you want to do in this country," I said.

Just then a sweet peace came over me, His peace. I believe it blessed the Lord for me to care more for the souls than for my comfort or transportation. Now, it's nice to have a new vehicle you don't have to work on every day, you know; but that wasn't what I was concerned about. It pleases the Father when we put Him first.

It wasn't easy for Jesus to leave Heaven and come down here and walk in our shoes, and go through all He went through. He wasn't looking for the easy route; He did it all for our salvation.

I came back and said, "Okay, brother, I can accept it now."

So they did that, they bought this brand new pickup, and drove it out.

Then that same brother said, "I've got a camper that will fit right on there, one of these overhead campers that doesn't have anything in it."

"That's exactly what I want, I don't want anything in it, because I might be hauling 15 or 20 people in it before it's over," I said.

"Stop by my place, and we'll put the camper on," he said.

We stopped by his place and put the camper on. This was a red truck with a white camper. Boy oh boy, was I sticking out.

When we had traveled further, another brother said, "I've got a little flat bottom aluminum boat I want to give you."

So we strapped it on top. You talk about a tourist looking guy now; I look like I'm fisherman number one. I am. I'm fishing for men, fishing for souls.

So the Lord provided that truck. Over all those roads and all the things we put it through, that truck held up for nineteen years in Belize! The blessing of the Lord was on that truck. That was the truck with the big speakers on top and we would go down the road playing gospel music.

Delivering Bibles

On the return trip in the new truck, we were given a whole lot of Bibles. I was so anxious to get there to take them to these people that had never seen Bibles. Many of them had accepted the Lord, but they needed the Word. So we arrived at Belize, and started to go down south toward some of the most remote villages there. What they had for roads would not be considered roads here. We put our truck in four-wheel drive and we just went right through. We got way down there in the bushes, and were miles from anywhere, when we got stuck!

This mud hole was about a hundred yards long, and it had several sets of big ruts through it. If I had some of the big tires I see nowadays, I could have made it through. I had pretty good tires, but they weren't high enough. So I was finally able to back up and get out. Then we started looking for a path or some way we could get through this stretch of mud. We picked out a path up on top of the ruts. We took some little sticks that we cut with our machetes to lie on the path so that when we got started again, we could make it through. We got right out in the middle of the mud hole and slipped right off into another rut and was sucked down. The back of the truck was in the mud, and we were stuck there.

So I got out, and began wading around in the mud trying to figure out how I was going to get out. My dad was sitting in the truck; grumbling. We all have flesh to conquer.

He was grumbling, "If it had been me, I wouldn't have gone out here in the first place," he was saying.

He forgot that when I was a little boy back in Arkansas in those rice fields, there were bad roads too. At that time he was driving and I was the one putting planks under the wheels trying to get us out. He didn't even get out of the truck.

"Dad, just take one look out that window and tell me what you see," I told him.

He looked out there, "I don't see nothing but a bunch of deep ruts," he said.

"Do you know what that tells me?" I asked. "That tells me that there has been somebody here before us and they are not still here. We are miles into the jungle, and there isn't anyone around. That tells me that people have been stuck here before and they aren't anymore. So we are *not* going to stay in here. We're on a mission and we are going on."

The Lord promised me when I was a young man on a school ground when I didn't know anybody and I felt like I had no friends, that He would be my friend and would not leave or forsake me.

So I said, "Jesus; here we are, stuck in this mud until You get ready to go. You said You wouldn't go off and leave me, so You are stuck in the mud with me."

What is faith anyway? Faith believes that God meant what He said. He doesn't just meet us in church; He meets with us out in the mud hole too. We are supposed to rejoice in Him when we have plenty and when we don't. He is the God of everything. So my attitude was just to worship God; that's all I could do. We didn't have any 911 or AAA to call; so we stayed there all night long fighting all the bugs and animals.

At about ten o'clock the next morning I heard a rumbling noise way in the background. It kept getting a little closer. It turned out to be one of those huge, high-wheeled army trucks. The British Army was coming to get us out. God knew where they were, and He knew where we were. The truck was loaded with men because they were on maneuvers. They got there, stopped, and started laughing at us for having our brand new truck stuck in the mud. They all got out of the truck, and I went over to talk to their captain. I told him about the set of ruts on the other side and said that if he would take those ruts, he could go on through; but since I was the one stuck there, he didn't want to listen to me. He didn't know that I had hours to investigate it. So he got stuck in a set of ruts himself. He didn't even get as far as I was, before his big truck was stuck too. Now they were stuck in the mud and they weren't laughing after that. I had our truck equipped with big speakers, one on the front and one on the back, so I turned on the gospel music. I had a captive audience now, so I let Jesus talk to them in song.

They decided to take their wench and hook it onto our truck and a tree and pull me out of there with the wench; but the wench broke. All the while I was still praising God. After a while I heard another rumbling noise. It was the British Forest Service driving a truck just like the one before, given to them by the British Army. When they got there they stopped on the other side of the mud hole. They took a big cable and pulled that big army truck out. So I told them that if they checked out the set of ruts on the other side, they could go through. Still, they wouldn't listen to me; and again, they sunk their big truck deep in the mud before they got as far as I was. They had to pull them back out, and finally the hard headed captain decided to try those ruts, and they got right through.

The Lord's way doesn't always agree with our way. When we get too smart, sometimes we miss God's way. We think we have it figured out, but He knows the way.

So they got through, and then hooked the long cable to our truck, and the Lord got us out.

I didn't fail the test. Have you ever failed one of God's tests? Sometimes we're in a place where God is doing something in our lives and we grumble and complain. When we act like that, we don't bring any glory to God. He isn't blessed in those situations, and we don't bless other people either. The Lord wants us to give thanks in everything. He said He would not leave us, and He won't. He will do what He said He would do.

Bring Them to Jesus

When He asked me to go to Belize, He didn't ask me if I wanted to go, He told me He wanted to go. Personally, I did not want to go. God was moving in such a powerful way in the church in Arizona, you never knew what God was going to do. Besides, I didn't know anybody in that country. Why would I want to go there? But Jesus did. He knew many people that needed Him, and just asked me, will you go with Me?

You know that little song that we sing sometime, "I'll go where You want me to go, I'll do what You want me to do, and I'll say what You want me to say."

We are in a harvest field today. I believe this is the end-time harvest, don't you? There are people out there who need Jesus. They don't need preaching to, they don't need to be condemned; they need Jesus to lift them up. He will lift them out of the horrible place where Satan has brought them into captivity. They need lifting.

As I look back over the years and all the places that the Lord sent us throughout that country, I am thankful to be a part of the Lord's great work there. Many souls have already gone on to be with the Lord and the ones that remain are carrying the torch. The Gospel is going forth from Belize. Not only in that country, but sending missionaries out of Belize into Cuba and over into Africa and other places. This is what the Gospel is intended to do; touch the lives and hearts of people and bring them to Jesus. Then He does His wonderful work of redemption and regeneration.

He Heals and Saves

I think so often of Jesus as He was teaching in this place and the house was packed. There was a man that really needed a touch from the Lord, but he couldn't get there. So these four men had compassion on him, and they put him on some kind of a stretcher thing and carried him to Jesus.

You know, I really believe what they said was, "If we can just get him to Jesus, we won't have to carry him back."

When they got there, they couldn't even get in the house, there were so many people.

So they said, "Well, we've only got one other thing to do, and that's take the roof off."

I don't know how they got him up there, and I don't know how they got the roof off, but I know they let him down right in front of Jesus. The first thing Jesus said was, *"Son, thy sins are forgiven thee"* (Mark 2:5).

So he must have been a sinner. But these men had compassion on him; they loved him enough to get him to Jesus.

"If we can just get him to Jesus, we won't have to carry him back!"

And Jesus said, *"Thy sins are forgiven thee, arise, take up your bed and walk"* (Mark 2:9-11). Hallelujah!

Do you believe that today? I believe if we can get people to Jesus, He will take care of what ever they need, but we need to bring them to Jesus. It's worth it; in the grocery store, in the gas station, in the business offices, just allow Jesus to shine through you.

Praise Brings a Better Answer

One time I remember we needed a vehicle for the work of the Lord. That's when I Pastored out in Globe, Arizona. I had driven all over Phoenix, looking for a vehicle that we could afford to buy. I had almost given up when I stopped in this last little place before going back to Globe.

I saw this car sitting there, and the Holy Spirit said, "That's the one right there!"

Now whenever I'm going to buy a vehicle, I want to test it out a little, you know, check under the hood, drive it around the block and check it out. The salesman came out.

I stopped and was looking at it, "Do you want to drive it?" he asked.

"No, I don't need to drive it, I want that car right there," I answered.

I tell you, when the Lord tells you that's it, then that is it!

"No, man, you need to drive it," he insisted.

"Okay, okay," I replied.

So I drove around the block and came back, "Yep, that's the one I want," I said.

We went in his office and he told me how much he wanted for the car. Well, it was way more than I had.

"Well sir, I don't have that much." I told him. "We need a van up in Globe, for the church, and that's what we're looking for. I just don't have that much, this is how much I have."

I showed him the amount I had.

"Well no, we couldn't take that for this car," he said.

All of a sudden, it was like the Holy Ghost just rose up inside of me. I'm not usually given to emotion, but I turned around and started jumping up and down and praising God! Because God already said that was the car, so just because he said, "No." It didn't mean no.

The brothers that were with me later said, "You should have seen that guy's face when you started jumping up and down and praising God."

"Well, if people can curse and swear, give me equal time to praise God!" I told them.

If the world can be so bold to carry on their filthy ways, then just give me equal time to praise God.

When I got through praising God, I looked back at him, "You can have the car, man, you can have the car!" he said.

Does it pay to praise the Lord? Absolutely! It's not hard to praise the Lord when you come to church, but when you're out there where things come against you, and you're more or less standing alone, that's the time that you need to praise the Lord. He's always there. So let's just be faithful to Jesus, don't be ashamed of Him. The world is not ashamed to carry on their foolishness and their ungodly ways, so we're not ashamed of Jesus.

Once I saw a man walking down the sidewalk, carrying a sign that read, "I'm a fool for Christ," and on his back another one that read, "Whose fool are you?"

So, we're not trying to act foolish, but we're trying to magnify the Lord and exalt Him, because He is the answer. Praise God!

Chapter 7

Continuing to Share Jesus

Wait for the Promise

I really feel like this is a very, very important time that we're living in. It is an important time, not only to God, but to the world and to all of us as believers. Jesus, the best teacher that the world has ever known, hand picked his disciples and taught them personally. Wouldn't you like to know all the things that He taught and shared with them? Thank God for what we have recorded, but when it was all about to end as they knew it, and a new beginning, the whole responsibility of God's plan in the earth was about to be placed in the hands of twelve men.

He said, *"Go into all the world and preach the Gospel to every creature. He who believes and is baptized will be saved; but he who does not believe will be condemned"* (Mark 16:15-16 NKJV).

He told them, "Don't even go until you've been endued with power from on high, because you are My witnesses," (See, Acts 1:4-5).

When Jesus was here He walked in the power of the Holy Ghost. The disciples walked with Him and watched Him as He did the great works of the Father.

"Now you are going to carry on these works. You are My representatives in the earth. This is the way people will know that I have been resurrected; when they see the same works that I did among you, being done, they are going to know that I am living and that I'm living in you and that you are my chosen ones," He said.

They did exactly what He said. How many would like to go and just sit down in a place and wait for ten days? You don't go to work, you don't eat, and you just wait. You know waiting is one of the hardest things for us to do, isn't it? We want it yesterday. It just can't come quick enough.

"I have promised that in the last days I will pour out of My Spirit" (See Joel 2:28-29).

"You wait for the promise," Jesus said.

You know that word "days" has an "S" on it which means plural. We are still living in those last days. We are in the last of the last days. If the disciples that Jesus chose and trained did all those wonderful miracles and needed the power of the Holy Ghost to carry on the work of God, how much more do we need it in these days?

It's not by might, it's not by education, it's not by how many Scriptures we can quote, but He said, *"It's by My Spirit, saith the Lord"* (Zech. 4:6).

Where God's Spirit is there is liberty, freedom, deliverance, healing and restoration. All the good things you could talk about are in His presence.

The Anointing

When the Lord called me into the ministry and sent us out we were pastoring a little church in North Little Rock, Arkansas, in a little community out there. We had left our new home, never slept one night in it. Forsook all to follow Jesus and do what He said do.

I remember one night after service I just felt like I needed more. You feel that way sometimes. We all do don't we? So I just stayed in the church and went in the little office and was just praying and waiting before the Lord. The Lord came to me and made me to know that He had seen all that I left behind just like His disciples of old did. They left everything and followed Jesus.

He came to me so sweetly, and said, "Just ask whatever you want, and I will give it to you."

God doesn't play tricks, and He is not in the business of fooling around, He means business. So I believed that He meant just what He said!

I searched my heart for a moment and with all my heart I said, "God, what I really, really want is more of your anointing in my life."

The anointing of God, His presence; not just when we come to church, but at all times. Everywhere; in the gas stations, in the grocery stores, in the business places; wherever.

"Lord, I just want more of that anointing," I said.

The Bible said, *"The yolk is destroyed because of the anointing"* (Isa. 10:27).

It's not just one time being filled with His Spirit. The Bible gives us examples of many places in the New Testament where they were refilled. They were continually being filled, Praise God, staying filled. Did you know that the Lord is coming for a church that is filled with His Spirit? What do you think is going to propel you off of this ground when Jesus comes? It is going to have to be the Spirit of God in us!

I've seen on television where they've made some kind of a rocket type thing. They strap it on somebody, turn it on and, whoosh— it'll shoot them up in the air. We're not going to have rockets on the outside just the Holy Ghost on the inside. But the enemy is out to destroy people, our country, and anything that's good. There is only one thing that can stop him from working, and that's the power of the Holy Ghost and the Word of God. That will stop him in his tracks. The Lord is looking for a church that is filled with His Spirit. Praise the Lord!

Shelter in the Storm

One time in Belize we were in a village way down south and the radio had begun broadcasting that there was a terrible hurricane headed in that direction. If we went further south, that would be more in the path of the hurricane, but to go back toward our home was very dense jungles; and just a trail of a road made through the jungles.

So we prayed and ask God, "Which direction do we need to go?"

He really dealt with our hearts that we needed to go north. That was back toward where we lived. So we started out. We hadn't gone very far until the hurricane caught up with us and there we were in this dense jungle with trees being blown down. In the forest when those hurricane winds come through, they just topple trees of all kinds. Huge trees were falling all around us. Now what are you going to do in a case like that?

Wasn't it David that said, *"What time I am afraid, I will trust in Thee"* (Ps. 56:3)?

Does that mean that fear never comes to any of us? No, it does come. It comes to all of us sometimes. Sudden fear sometimes comes to you, but when that fear comes, we put our trust in Jesus who knows all about us and where we are and what we need. We put our trust in His protection.

"He who dwelleth in the secret place of the Most High shall abide under the shadow of the Almighty" (Ps. 91:1).

Praise God! His presence is there! Hallelujah!

We heard the trees falling and just kept going. Finally they fell in front of us and we had a four-wheel drive truck, but we had to get out and chop our way through to get over the logs and on through, for mile after mile.

Why am I sharing these things? I want us to know and be aware that our God is with us. He is with us. Wherever we are, that's where He is. When we come together, we bring Him with us, praise God, His presence is there.

There is a Scripture in first Chronicles, chapter 16 and verse 8; and this is what it says, *"Give thanks unto the Lord, call upon His name; make known His deeds among the people."*

That is exactly what this book is all about--to make known His deeds, not our deeds; but His deeds. All He expects from us is to believe Him and to trust Him. When we do that He will manifest Himself.

When we got through mile after mile of these things happening; in the natural, it is really scary, because you never know when one of those huge trees that's been there for years and years is going to come tumbling down on you.

It is in times like those that we trust in the Lord. I'm talking about something that's real. I'm not talking about religion or doctrine. I'm talking about life in Christ.

Paul said, *"the life which I now live in the flesh I live by the faith of the Son of God"* (Gal. 2:20).

It's His faith, and I live by it. His faith will always conquer. His faith will bring you through with victory on the other side.

I'll never forget when we finally got out of the jungle area we had the radio playing, and they said, "The Humming Bird Highway is closed."

I said, "Yes sir, it surely is," because we had just come through there.

The Lord knows exactly where we are, and He knows how to protect us when we trust in Him.

"What time I am afraid, I will trust in Thee" (Ps. 56:3).

I will trust in the Lord. That's a choice, that's our choice, and if we trust in Him, He will deliver us!

A Desperate Cry

At another time we were at a village on the island of Placencia having a revival and the whole family was there. We had reached this village in our speedboat. We had a sixteen foot speedboat with a 50 horsepower Mercury engine. We were there having meetings. After the crusade I wanted to take my family home and we got weathered in and it wasn't safe to take them back by speedboat the same way we came in. So this young man that was sailing the sailboat when we should have gone down in the sea was with me piloting this little speedboat. I just really felt like we should go back up to the village where we keep the boat and then from there we would get the pick-up, and go around and come back and pick up the family. When we got out on the sea it was very rough. There were huge breakers and we were going right into them. If you didn't know how to operate the boat, the wave would come and, BAM; the bottom would just drop out from under you, and the next wave would come.

He finally said, "Brother Samuel, it is really not safe to be out here."

It was several miles up the sea to where we were going to go.

So we turned back, and I could not rest, because something in me was saying, "You've got to go, you've got to go."

Now, I'm not a brave man in the natural, but when God puts it on you so strong; then you know this is what He wants.

I asked this brother, "Do you think there is any possible way that we could make it up there, and go up the river to that village?"

"Well, like I told you, it is very dangerous, but if you think we ought to go; then let's just go." he answered.

So we got back out on that sea; and I'm telling you, it felt like every bone in your body would shatter, because those waves would bring us up, and then just drop us, BAM, back down hard. Then if you didn't watch out, the next one would break over on top of you and sink you. We did that for a long time, I don't know, several hours we did that, fighting those waves to get up to the river. When we got to where the river empties out to the sea, of course, the river was smooth. Oh my, it felt good to sit in that boat and cruse up the river.

We were just cruising along probably about 30 miles an hour when we passed this last house that is on that river before it empties out into the sea. There was a man standing out on his little dock that reached out over the river, waving at us. Well, I thought he was just waving at us, so I waved back at him. But as we went by he was gesturing with his arms, and in their language that means, help or stop.

"Brother! We've got to go back, he needs something," I said.

So we turned around and went back. As we drove up to his dock and got out, you could see the look of relief on his face.

"What is wrong, Brother?" I inquired.

The man answered, "My wife is in the house, unconscious; but the last words she said before she went unconscious were, 'God, send brother Hooper to pray for me.'"

She had no idea in the world where I was in that country and it really didn't matter to her. All she knew was, if God would send brother Hooper to pray, she would be well! Now I knew why I couldn't stay in that village. I knew now why the Holy Ghost kept prompting me to go anyway. Take the chance of dying in that sea, being overcome of the waves--go anyway! So we went in where she was, and she was lying there unconscious.

"She has been so sick and she's dying, but God heard her last words," her husband said.

I replied, "Yes, God heard her last words."

We think sometimes that because we don't get an answer right away that God didn't hear when we ask Him, but He did! His ear is not heavy that He can't hear, and His arm is not short that He can't reach you.

You might say, "Well, she's just a little insignificant woman living down there on the river. God is not paying that much attention to her. He is watching over all those big TV Evangelists and all those well known men and women who are doing great things for God."

But He is watching the very least one who cries out to Him. He hears them! So when we went in, there wasn't a doubt in my mind that God was not going to raise that woman up. God heard her prayer, He sent us there, and He is going to do what He said He would do. So even though she was unconscious, we prayed asking God to touch this woman. Then we began to praise God for the victory! All the while we were praising God, because I know God is doing this. It is not me, it's Him. We are not the one that performs the miracles, it is Him! We just obey what He says, and then He does the work.

So I began to speak to this woman.

"You will live, you will live!" I said.

She opened her eyes and saw us there and oh my goodness, you should have seen the biggest ol' smile all over her face, because Jesus had answered her prayer. Did you know God delights in answering our prayers? We say, we don't think so sometimes because it doesn't happen instantly, but God does hear you, and He will answer you, when you cry out of desperation. He also will answer you in the way that will meet your need.

I told her, "Sister, we are going on up the river. We're going to go get my truck, go around the other direction and take another little boat across the lagoon, get my family, and we will be back. I will be back at your house here by 5:00 o'clock tonight, because you are well."

So we got in the boat, went on up the river and I went around like I said. We went over and got the family and brought them back. We all came back down the river to her house and got there at exactly 5:00 o'clock. There she was sitting out on the front porch, rocking and singing! Hallelujah! The Lord wants His deeds to be known. Those are the things that are really important.

God Breaks a Curse

There was a woman when we first went into those areas who had several miscarriages. She could not have a child because a spell had been cast upon her. In that area there was another woman who was jealous of her and got this witch doctor to cast a spell on her. The spell was to prevent her from ever being able to have children.

Now these things are real. Did you know Satan has power? Do you know what opens the door to him? It's fear. Fear opens the door to the enemy.

We learned about this when she came to the meetings.

"Do you think that God can set me free?" she asked.

"No, I don't think, I know. I know He can set you free, because that's what He came to do, to set the captives free!" I answered.

So we prayed, rebuked that enemy, and commanded her body to reproduce, as God intended for a mother to do. Not long after that, she got in "a family way," as they said back when I was a young man. Did you know she went on to have three beautiful children? Hallelujah!

Jesus breaks every fetter! Praise God!

This is what causes people that don't know Christ to really want to know Him, when they see the goodness of the Lord. When they see Him in operation and see His Spirit working and moving. A lot of people don't know how to describe the presence of God, but when it is there they can feel it! I've walked up and down in pastures and cows on the other side of the fence would follow me. I'd be there walking, praying and praising God and they would just go right with me on the other side of the fence. They didn't know what I was saying or anything else but they could feel the presence of God.

"1 Will Bring You Down"

We had a wonderful experience while we were in Belize with the Chief Administrator and the Chief Engineer from NASA in Houston, Texas. They came and visited us in our home one day. They were curious how we lived and operated in Belize.

You know, it shouldn't be; but it's kind of a shame in some cases to tell people that you are a faith missionary, because many come and say God sent them to do all these great works, and in a short time they are back in the states. It's sad. So I stopped and thought for a moment. Should I just go ahead and tell them the truth? Yeah, I'll tell them the truth.

"We live by faith," I said.

They asked, "Yeah, but who supports you?"

I replied, "Jesus."

"How do you get your support, how can you live here?"

You know, they saw the missionary equipment, the place where we lived, and what we did there, and they were thoroughly impressed.

"Well, the Lord asked me if I would go with Him to this country, and I just came down here to bring Him down here. I'm not here to build a Kingdom, a great ministry, or a name; I'm here to bring Jesus to these people. That is what I'm here for, and because I'm here in His will, He supplies our needs," I said.

I thought, "Uh-huh; yeah, they probably are going to really look down their noses at me."

To my amazement they said, "That's the way it ought to be."

You know why they could say that? They could say that because they had a real experience with God in operation at NASA Space Center. Do you remember when Apollo 13 was lost in space? Do you remember those days way back then? Their spacecraft was lost. Lost, meaning there was no connection to bring it back to the earth. They have a limited amount of oxygen and supplies on board those spacecraft, and if they don't get back;

they are buried in space. The time had come very close to their limitation, and they were working around the clock trying to get control of this spacecraft to bring it back to the Earth, and they couldn't do it. No matter what they did, they could *not* get control of that aircraft to bring it back. So finally they decided that the best thing to do was to go home, get an hour or two of sleep; eat something, get refreshed and come back, and maybe their mind would be clearer.

So they did that, and when they came back together, one of the men said, "You know, I had the strangest thing happen to me while I slept. I had a dream, and in this dream, we did this, and this; and this, to the spacecraft, got control of it and brought it back!"

The big shots said, "Well, you know, that's old fogy stuff, which was back in Daniel's days, he dreamed those dreams and people back then did that, but we're smart, we have education, we know what we are doing."

They wouldn't listen to him and they just kept on, and kept on, trying different things. Nothing they tried was working.

Finally they came to themselves. Like the prodigal's son did, he came to himself.

Then they said to this man, "Well, we haven't been able to do anything, so why don't we just try what you saw in your dream."

So they did exactly the steps that God had shown this man in the dream. It proved to work and they knew it must be God. They got control of the spacecraft and brought it back and landed it. Do you know what happened at NASA Space Center? A revival broke out! Because God proved to them that He was smarter than they were.

God is smarter than the smartest of our day. The most knowledgeable scientist doesn't hold a light to a Holy Ghost filled believer. We may not be smart in book learning and all these scientific things, but those that know God are the wise ones.

Daniel said, *"but the people that do know their God shall be strong, and do exploits"* (Dan. 11:32).

But that knowing part is what I'm talking about, that's in the Spirit realm; knowing God, being filled with His Spirit.

"For as many as are led by the Spirit of God, they are the sons of God" (Rom. 8:14).

If you are a child of God then you have power and authority, by His Spirit that dwells in you. Is God looking for a church like that today? Absolutely!

What is going to convince this heathen unbelieving world that we live in today that God is real? The manifestations of God are going to convince them.

So they told how that when they realized that God was greater than they were, they began to humble themselves, and God began to move in their hearts and they began to accept the Lord and were filled with the Spirit! Revival broke out. Afterwards the Chief Administrator and the Chief Engineer were traveling to different countries letting people know that God is God!

When they first went into space I was kind of one of those critics; I thought, "Uh, they're messing around with God's territory up there. He put us down here; he didn't make man to go up there."

I just kind of believed that they never would make it.

Then when they made it to the moon, I said, "Now, wait a minute, maybe I'd better take another look."

So I found in the Scripture where it says, *"and though you set your nest among the stars, from there will I bring you down, says the Lord"* (Obad. 4 NKJV).

Then I said to the Lord, "Oh, You knew that all the time, didn't You? You knew they were going to do this."

Then I began to see something else, because for some reason, a few years ago, people that knew Christ and followed the Lord, were looked down upon. "They're just using God as a crutch, because they are ignorant, and they're not smart enough to make it on their own," they would say.

They looked down on people that really knew and followed Christ.

So what God did was, He took the very much trained and educated people, let them go to the moon, and come back and proved to them that He was real!"

So then they couldn't say it was just for the poor, the ignorant and the uneducated. God is doing everything He can to reach everybody in our world today. He has taken men of low degree and elevated them up. He has taking men of high degree and brought them down.

God wants us to know that, "I am your God, I am your Father, and I love you."

Even when we are unlovable, He still loves us.

So there they were; people that at one time didn't even believe God, thought they were smarter than God, traveling around the world, going to different nations being missionaries for God! He just let them come by our house so that we could hear their testimony of God in operation and be blessed also. Hallelujah!

Missionary Trip to Mexico

I want the Lord to be magnified in everything I say and do, because in myself, I am nothing. It doesn't matter if I gave my heart to Him when I was seven years old and never went out in sin, that doesn't make me special. I know if we walk humbly with the Lord and give Him the credit and the glory for what He does, He'll do greater things. It's not hard for Him to perform miracles.

One of our first mission trips was in Mexico in 1961. A missionary I had known for many years in Mexico kept inviting me to come down.

I would answer, "I didn't loose anything down there."

I wasn't looking forward to taking a mission trip to Mexico, but God kept dealing with me to go.

"But Lord, I don't have the money to make a trip like that," I said.

I'm going to confess something, we all fail sometimes.

"Lord, if You really want me to go, send in the money, and I'll go," I replied.

God sent the money in, but about that time school had started and we had children that needed school supplies and clothes. So I spent that money buying school clothes, books, and things for the children to go to school. You'd think the Lord would just grab me up and paddle me good, wouldn't you? No, He didn't. Do you know what He said?

I heard, "I still want you to go."

"But Lord, I don't have the money anymore, I spent it," I answered.

I didn't do it wastefully, I had a good excuse.

"Well, you know, that isn't hard for Me, I'll do it again," the Lord said.

So He sent it in again, a whole hundred dollars. Can you make that trip down there and back on a hundred dollars? God still knows how to stretch money, gasoline, and food, whatever you need.

So we left and went down to this town in Mexico. Way down below Mexico City in this town of Iguala is where the Lord was sending us. Two brothers and I went in my Dodge pickup truck. We just kept driving and driving and it felt like we would never get there. The further we went and the deeper we got into Mexico, my eyes began to get red, bloodshot, because we didn't stop to sleep.

This one brother said, "You rest and I'll drive."

I'll tell you what, I couldn't rest the way he drove.

So we finally made it there, and I said, "Oh God, what in the world am I doing here? I can't speak their language. I don't have any idea why I'm here. Why am I here?"

They were having a home meeting that night. It was kind of a fellowship and prayer meeting; in a native's home.

The brother that we went to be with said, "Brother Samuel, what do you want to do?"

"Why don't we just pray," I replied.

I felt like I needed a spiritual infusion and renewed physical strength. As we began to pray the Spirit of the Lord began to move and then I began to feel better. I wasn't supposed to share or do anything with them that night, so I just went. My eyes were just red, hurting, and bloodshot real bad. When I got there the people didn't know me or anything about me, but the love and compassion of God just flowed out of them. They began to pray in Spanish and I didn't understand many of the words they were saying, but God healed my eyes. He healed my eyes and just made me feel right at home.

Unusual Message

We had a citywide meeting, and one night the Lord began to deal with me.

The subject was, "What great things you must suffer for My name's sake."

"Lord, if I preach that, who would want to follow You? Who would come and give their heart to You, if I preach on, 'You're going to have to suffer if you follow Jesus?'" I asked.

But the Spirit would not let me off. So we got to the meeting and had to preach through an interpreter.

We were preaching and sharing, "What great things you will suffer."

This is what the Lord told Saul of Tarsus, wasn't it? *"What great things you will suffer"* (Acts 9:16), and he did.

Then as we finished I made an alter call, and said, "Everyone that would really like to accept Christ, would you come forward?"

To my amazement people began to come forward.

They're predominately Catholic and they are always taught to kneel. They don't ever stand and pray, they kneel. They came and began to kneel.

I'll never forget, this one lady said, through an interpreter, "I can't kneel because my knees are so physically bad, I just can't kneel."

"Jesus can take care of that," I said.

We laid our hands on her, God healed her, and down on her knees she went, and accepted the Lord! Every night, every place we went the Lord touched people's hearts, and they would come and give their heart to Jesus.

As we were in this citywide campaign, we were playing our instruments and really getting in the Spirit, getting ready to let God use us. If you are going to go out, you usually go get in the shower, put on your best clothes, and get ready to go. Well there's a time when I think we need to get ready to meet the Lord, get prepared, spend time with Him, just soak in His love, His Spirit, His presence. So that when we come into the house of the Lord, we bring Him with us and we are ready to flow. We don't have to be pumped up.

Did you ever use an old pump with a handle? Sometimes you have to pour water in it and prime it before it will work.

That's what we have to do sometimes in church, prime the pump. But when you come in, when you have spent time before the Lord and come into His house, nobody has to pump the handle; it just flows.

The Spirit's Warning

So we were in this missionary's home worshiping and praising God and playing our guitars, and all of a sudden the Lord spoke urgently to me, "Go outside!"

Well, the place where this missionary lived, the front of his house fit right up against the sidewalk in town.

So I laid the guitar down, walked outside and all the while I was thinking, "What am I doing out here?"

I walked down the sidewalk a little ways, still nothing.

"Lord, what am I doing out here?" I asked.

As I walked back past my truck, I discovered there was a huge fire that had been placed under the bottom of my truck! Immediately I began to get the wood and stuff they had put under there to set it on fire, out from under the truck. About that time a young man came walking down the street that belonged there and noticed what was happening. He ran into the missionary's house and told him what was going on, and he came running out there.

If I had not gone out when the Lord told me to, that truck would have burned to the ground. It had two gas tanks on it and both were full. There's no telling what would have happened. Obedience is something the Lord is teaching us, isn't He? He is teaching us to be led of the Spirit and just be obedient.

So we got the fire out. This brother didn't rest until he inquired and searched around and finally found out who did it. It was two young men.

So we found them and asked, "Why did you do that?"

They told us that the priest put them up to it. The priest told them that they would be doing God a favor if they would burn up this "gringo" preacher's truck.

So he began to explain to them, "You didn't realize it, but that truck had two gas tanks on it, and they were both full. If that truck had caught on fire and exploded, no telling how many blocks of this town would have burned down!"

But these are the things that the Lord lets us know; "I know all about you, I know where you are, and I know what you need; just be obedient."

Hot Peppers Cooled

We went to one very remote village and there was a huge river that went down close to their village. The church there had suffered much persecution. People even burned the church building down one time. Before the service they wanted to treat us and had a time of fellowship. Do you know what they treated us with? They treated us with what they had, frijoles and tortillas. In case you don't know what frijoles are, they are beans. Served with a big bowl of hot sauce. They like that hot pepper. We were sitting there visiting and had a little tin dish of a thing and no spoon. You dip your tortilla down, and dip it out; manners go out the door.

I'll never forget, I was telling this brother, "I sure would love to hear some of these people testify because I know God has done some great things for them. I would love to hear their testimonies."

Everywhere we went, of course, they wanted the "gringos" to speak. So while I was telling this brother that, I didn't realize that I was dipping the only spoon on the table with hot sauce into my beans.

I guess I had about three spoons of it in there already, and this brother said, "Brother Samuel, you might want to hold up a little, that hot sauce really is hot."

I'm not really hot on hot sauce. I can take a little mild, but not really hot sauce. If you don't eat the food they give you, they feel like you think you're better than they are. Now I'm in a dilemma. If I leave it, I'm going to leave a bad impression. If I eat it, I'm going to be smoking out my ears.

So let me tell you what I did. The Lord always knows, you never can back Him up in a corner. The Lord always knows what our situation is, and even if we got ourselves into that situation, He can get us out.

So this is what I did. I just stopped right there, and prayed again. How many times do you pray over your food? Sometimes I pray over mine two, three or four times, when I'm eating certain food.

Well, I prayed again, and said, "Lord, You're the same One who took the fire out of the fiery furnace for the three Hebrew children, and if You did that for them, You can take the fire out of this hot sauce for me."

Did He do it? Oh yes He did. I ate it and felt no ill effect!

The Blood of Jesus Has Power

We got into the service and people began worshiping God. All of a sudden, a little lady stood up, about half-way back in the congregation. Her little eight year old daughter stood up along side of her and she began to testify. Well, I thought maybe they had mentioned to the people to do that, because they say a lot of words in Spanish and I don't know what they're talking about. So I thought maybe they had mentioned that if someone in here has a testimony, to give it, but nobody had. There hadn't been any requests for testimonies.

The little church was packed that night. Some of the worst guys in the whole village, probably some of the ones that burned the church down, came to see these "gringos." We were way, way back in there; we were not around where tourists are, so we looked funny to them. They came to see the "gringos." They didn't get to see much of us, because I want you to know, God manifested Himself in that place!

A little mother stood up to give her testimony. The missionary brother was interpreting from Spanish to English, so we could understand what she was saying, and her little eight year old daughter stood up with her to bear witness.

She said, "Not too long ago my little daughter came to me," and said, "Mama, we don't have any water."

Of course they have big families and a lot of children. Her mama was busy with the rest of the children, and didn't notice this little girl take the bucket and go to the river to get some water. That's where they got their water, out of the river.

When she got there the bank was pretty steep and the river was real deep, and when she reached over to get the water she slipped and fell into the river.

Now, as Christians, it is important that we teach our children the power of God.

I have heard that you always come up about three times before you drown. I never have drowned so I guess that's true. Anyway, the first time she came up, she yelled, "THE BLOOD OF JESUS HAS POWER!" and down she went again. The second time she came up, she yelled, "THE BLOOD OF JESUS HAS POWER!" Down she went again. The third time she came up standing on the bank with a full bucket of water in her hand! Then she ran to tell her mother what Jesus had done for her! Glory to God!

Bad Tooth Pulled

Another little lady stood up and said, "You know, a few days ago God did something for me. I had a bad tooth that was hurting so bad."

It's not easy to get to the Dentist there. You have to go across the river and travel many miles, and of course it cost money.

She said, "I just could not get to the Dentist. I laid down the other night on the bed with my head on the pillow, and said, 'Jesus, You put that tooth in there, You can take it out!' I woke up the next morning; no toothache, and there lay the tooth on the pillow beside me!"

Simple childlike faith is what God honors. We never got a chance to preach or anything. Some of the worst guys in the village that they had been praying for, the same ones they thought might have been responsible for burning the church down, came to the altar and gave their hearts to Jesus that night. Hallelujah!

God Got Us Home

There was also a manifestation of the works of the devil, because when I went to get in my truck, two of my tires were slashed with a knife! Two tires were flat. They had been slashed, you couldn't repair them. So when God works, the enemy works. But let me tell you, God is greater!

Then I remembered that before I left to go to Mexico, the Lord had told me, "Take an extra spare with you," and I realized why.

We jacked up the truck and put on the spare tire and the extra spare. I had to come all the way back to the United States without a spare tire. I don't even like to go across town without a spare tire.

But I said, "Lord, I did exactly what you said, and I believe that You will take care of the tires."

Quite awhile before we got out of Mexico the truck began to miss. You know their gas down there is not the octane like we have up here. It is better now but it used to be terrible. So the truck began to miss and didn't want to run. We had a long ways to go yet so we laid our hands on the dash of that truck, all three of us, and prayed for that old Dodge truck. Boy, it straightened up, perked up, and started running.

So when we got back into Texas we stopped at this little church and ministered and shared there. At that time the truck was running good.

"How is the truck running?" they asked.

"Well, it was missing, but it's running okay now," I said.

"Do you need us to work on it?" they inquired.

"No, it's okay, God took care of it," I replied.

It was quite a long way from the border back to North Little Rock, Arkansas. We got some good gas in the states, and I thought, "Well, you know, the truck has started running better now since we got good gas in it. It's okay."

After I got that Dodge pickup home it wouldn't even start the next morning!

So what did I have to do? I had to go buy a whole new set of spark plugs. I mean, those things were burnt to a crisp, but God brought us in. The Lord is the same, yesterday, today, tomorrow and forever. He doesn't change.

Do you know when the manna stopped for the children of Israel? After they crossed over Jordan, that's when the manna stopped. God provided a different way for them on the other side of the river than

He did in the wilderness. God provides for us here with good jobs, salaries, all the good food, and all of that. He provides for us, but, if it ever becomes necessary for us to be out there in the wilderness or somewhere and it's not there, He can provide manna again! He can multiply our food again. He can do it again. So, however He provides it is His provision, and all He wants from us is to use it and praise His name. Praise God!

Give and It Is Given

Quite some time ago, maybe two or three years ago, a brother friend of mine that had come down to Belize a few times to help us, had a truck that broke down on him there, a Dodge Cummins Diesel. Nobody could fix it, and it was bummed up here and there.

"We've got some good diesel mechanics in Texas," I told him.

So we put his truck on a trailer and I hooked it onto the back of my truck. Well, that truck was just as heavy as my truck so if I got up much speed it would start to wobble. I had to drive real slowly and it took me hours and hours of driving to get that truck back here and we began working on it.

Our Pastor and another brother helped me work on it. We began to trace out different problems and everything and over a period of time we finally pretty much diagnosed the problems and fixed them; but the thing was so bummed up. The brother that was helping me found another box, and we took the box off, and put the other one on. Then put a paint job on it, and got it going and everything; but it just would not sell. Now I'm talking about months; a couple of years or more, and it just wouldn't sell. I had quite a bit tied up in it too because the brother who owned the truck didn't have the money to put into it. So I would pitch in here and there, and was really fixing it for him. Today the truck sold!

Now, I'm not trying to play on anybody's sympathy, but for three days I have walked with only one dollar in my wallet. What can you buy with a dollar? It goes further than it used to, farther down the street before you can find anything to buy with it.

The only reason I'm telling you this is because I want you to know that God is still God. When it looks like there's no way out and it looks like there's no hope He can make a way. We lived in Belize for twenty-nine years solid and never wrote one letter asking anybody for an offering; not one newsletter. But God always provided. I want to tell you this thing is real. We've got a hold of something real, and we've just got a hold of the little end of something big! This thing is BIG; it's God!

Today this man came, and said, "I've been seeing that truck, and I've been asking God for it. Now I have the money and I have come for the truck."

He was a Christian man that works with the Gideons, but for quite awhile he didn't have the money to buy the truck. So now I have been repaid for what I did for the brother that owned the truck.

God Is My Source

One night recently in church some of us stood in the isle believing God for a financial miracle. I was one of those that stood.

The very next day a person that you wouldn't even believe would ever do something like that, called me and said, "Brother Hooper, I'm sending you a thousand dollars in the mail, you'll be getting a check."

Do you think God doesn't hear us? He hears us and He knows us.

When I first got to Belize that devil stood on my shoulder and just bore down on me.

"That faith life might work alright in the United States but it won't work down here," he said.

Do you know what I did? I laughed! I wasn't just putting on, I was laughing at him.

"Devil, don't you know who God is? He is the God of the Universe not just the God of the US!" I replied.

Do you know what he had to do? Whoosh—gone! He knows who God is.

Now, when I came up here he got on my shoulder again, and said, "Now, you're too old to work. You're not a missionary anymore. People won't provide for you so it won't work."

People always ask me, "When you get old and can't work anymore what are you going to do?"

That is a good question, but you know logic doesn't stand a chance with a miracle working God. You can't figure God out and how He's going to work, so just trust Him.

"When I can't get out there and work and do things, God will take care of us and He will do it His own way," I answered.

So what is Satan trying to do? He looks at where he thinks he can put fear in our heart, and fear opens the door for him to work. Just like faith opens the door for God to work. Fear nullifies faith, and then he has a place to get in. We wouldn't have to go take back what the devil stole from us if we never let him have it to start with!

"Neither give place to the devil" (Eph. 4:27).

He said just don't give him a place.

Jesus said, *"for the ruler of this world is coming, and he has nothing in Me"* (John 14:30 NKJV).

We can say that same thing. He doesn't have any place in us if we don't give him a place. We can resist the thoughts he brings to try to cause us to fear.

"Submit yourselves, therefore, to God. Resist the devil, and he will flee from you" (James 4:7).

Still on the Job

We came back to the states in 1995, doing exactly what the Lord wants me to do in this country too. A lot of people might think I'm not doing anything here, but I'm doing exactly what the Lord told me to do.

"Go everywhere and strengthen My people," He said. "You strengthen them and I'll straighten them. That's my job, I'm the Daddy, and I can handle that part."

The bad part is when children try to correct children, it doesn't work. It doesn't work in the home and it doesn't work in the church either. God knows how to deal with every one of us. When He corrects us, it works.

So that is what we're doing, we are going everywhere; no matter where it is, out on the street or wherever; whatever church. They asked me to preach in the Catholic Church, that big Catholic Church in Tyler, Texas. I went there and magnified Jesus. They ask me to preach in the First Methodist Church in Lindale. I go there and magnify Jesus. We go over to the Cowboy Church and magnify Jesus. In the business places, just magnify the Lord.

The Lord has given me a way to open a conversation around Him. You don't just jump in there and do that; sometimes you have to listen to them a little bit, follow the flow, and as the Lord works, you just insert something, and let the Lord grow it from there.

The Lord has called us to be His witnesses for this generation. We are God's light of the world. I don't know about you but I want my light to get brighter and brighter. I don't want it to flicker. I want it to get brighter.

As David said, *"Oh God, forsake me not, until I've shown thy strength unto this generation"* (Ps. 71:18).

We know the Lord is coming. We don't know when, but He said, *"Occupy 'till I come"* (Luke 19:13).

What did He mean by that? He meant to be about the Father's business. Do what He asks you to do. Be faithful to Him. Be faithful to worship God and bless God. Go to church and strengthen others. In so doing, you will be blessed and strengthened.

There are a lot of churches that need a touch from God.

When I drive by a church I pray, "God move in that church. Lord, reveal Yourself to the people. God, would you just show up and tell them who You are?"

It doesn't matter what is written over the door. So we just pray for them to let God move in their hearts.

Chapter 8

Only Believe

The Wings of an Eagle

I believe the secret to our personal victory is learning to praise the Lord. The Lord showed me that we are eagles. We are not chickens scratching around in the chicken pen looking up wishing we could be flying; we are eagles. He gave us the ability to soar.

I had a vision one time of an eagle sitting on a fence post. I've never seen that in real life because eagles just don't sit around on fence posts, but this eagle was sitting on a fence post and these young boys were coming along with rocks and stoning the eagle. He was being hurt very much by these stones.

I talked to this eagle and asked, "Why don't you fly? Because you could fly so high they could never reach you with those stones."

Then the Lord began to speak to me about praising Him. In everything give Him thanks, and then we can soar as the eagle. The storms that blow things away, the eagle uses it to ride and soar into the atmosphere. The Lord didn't put us under the circumstances, He put us over them. So He showed me that one wing of the eagle is prayer, and that's power. The other wing of the eagle is praise, and that is victory. If we pray a little, that gives us a little power; much prayer, much power. If we praise a little, we have a little victory; much praise, brings much victory! He has given us the wings of the eagle but guess what? We have to use them or we will find ourselves sitting on the fence post and everything that comes along hurts us. It really hurts when people say things and do things against you and treat you badly. You've treated them good and they turn around and render evil for good. It happens, doesn't it? But God gave us some wings. Let's use them and praise Him.

Everything that He has done, He will do, still can do, and wants to do.

The Scripture says, *"when the Son of man cometh, shall He find faith on the earth?"* (Luke 18:8).

It's a question, and my answer is, "Yes," because I'm going to believe, aren't you?

I'm going to say, "Yes, You are going to find faith on the earth, because I believe You and I believe Your Word."

I remember it was quite a struggle when we first went to Belize; and it wasn't my desire to go there, it was the Lord's desire. So when the Lord wants something done, He calls us to do what He wants to do. He's going to be with us, and He is going to show Himself strong on our behalf, but that doesn't mean that the adversary is not going to come against you. The adversary was there, and in much power; and determined to keep the will of the Lord from being done in that country.

But Jesus is Lord! As we acknowledge Him as Lord, He will defeat the enemy. No matter how he comes Jesus will defeat him. All Satan did for us was give us a brand new testimony.

Angels Watching

In Belize we started having services in that community out in a little lean-to that we built on the side of the house, just a little carport like thing. We were also having revival meetings all around, starting with having a little time of praising God and studying the Word. You know, when God wants to do something, there isn't always a big rush all at one time. He works us into it and enables us to do what He wants to do. So it looked kind of like the work was slow going for quite awhile.

Then we graduated into a tabernacle in a cow pasture. One of the brethren that was coming and became a part of the work there had a cow pasture, and we built a tabernacle; just a roof out in the cow pasture. Then as the Lord began to work and to move, we upgraded a little bit more and built a cement block church, with no ceiling in it. It had no windows, no fans, no air conditioning; but it was a place to worship God. There were times when we would be praising and worshiping the Lord, and people said they saw angels sitting up on the rafters. There was no ceiling, so there was just the two by fours going across there that holds the roof up; and they saw the angels hanging on, just really enjoying the presence of God. I thought, Lord, this is kind of strange. Then He made me to know why they were there. It doesn't matter whether you have a ceiling, or whether you don't, the angels rejoice when we worship God. The angels rejoice because if you could see around the throne right now, angels are worshiping God all around that throne.

They are missionary angels. They have been sent from heaven to earth to watch over us. I don't know if you have thought of it like that or not, but it's true. They've come to watch over and take care of us. You know they don't care a thing in the world about some dry programmed church service. That doesn't interest them one bit, but if they can find where people are really worshiping the Lord; that is where they congregate, because they feel at home there.

That's why the Scripture says, *"O Thou who inhabitest the praises of Israel"* (Ps. 22:3).

God just longs for that and loves that, and so do the angels. So when you worship God, even just a few, there are angels there. There are times when you just feel the presence of God so strong. Do you know what that is? That's not only the power of the Holy Spirit, that's the angels worshiping God with us. That's real, that's not a fairy tale; it is real. Hallelujah!

Tent Revival

So we kept praying and believing God and we finally decided to have a big tent meeting in our own village. Now, if you're going to have a tent meeting, you usually go to somebody else's town where they don't know you. But we set up this tent and told everybody we are going to have revival, and we did have revival. In the day time we would go to different homes, witnessing to people, telling them about Jesus and encourage them to come to the revival. Then have the meetings in the evening.

We saw God save some people that were hard, but God knows how to reach them. God began to move in a mighty way. In that tent revival there were at least a thousand people gathered there in these services; and we were just a little village way out in the boonies.

The anointing of the Holy Ghost was so powerful in that revival, that I saw young men that were walking on the highway, going by where we were having the tent meeting, come running in to the altar. Many of them before they ever got to the altar were "slain in the Spirit," like cord wood one on top of the other. There is absolutely no way that you could ever get this to happen; except by the presence of God. Just His presence melts the hearts of stone. There were people dancing in the isles, shouting, and praising God; others were being filled with the Spirit, and many were being saved. That is what

I call revival! It's not man made, its heaven sent; in answer to prayer. When God begins to move the devil has to take a back seat. He does not want to be around where the power of God is. He is darkness and he doesn't like light.

There were some; even some of the Christians around there, that said, "Oh, that's just a bunch of noise."

Well, God didn't think so. I've seen some get "slain in the Spirit," and they would become real "holy rollers;" just rolling all over the place. This is the way God began His work in Belize and thank God it is still going on today.

Missionary in Honduras

A few years before we were called to be missionaries in Belize, our missionary friend from Mexico and I had on our hearts for some time to visit a work that one of our missionary friends had started over in the country of Honduras, which borders Belize, on the south Caribbean Sea. This missionary had been there for about 18 months and had gone into these villages, witnessing for Christ; and teaching. From this ministry God had called a few young men that really gave their hearts to the Lord.

Later he and his family came out of Honduras to attend some meetings in the United States. They came by where we were way back up in the Ozark Mountains of Arkansas, having a tent meeting there; and they spent three days with us.

When we would sit down to eat he would cry.

We would ask, "What are you crying for, brother?"

"I just can't help but remember those poor, poor people where I came from; what they wouldn't give to sit down to a meal like this," He would reply.

His heart was just so touched for those people.

From Arkansas he and his wife were taking turns driving to a convention in California. She was driving now, and it was late at night.

She had asked him to stop and get a motel room, but he said, "No, we need to get there."

An eighteen-wheeler hit the back of that little Volkswagen bus they were driving and turned it end over end. The impact drove that engine into the gas tank and set it on fire!

I talked to the truck driver later and he told me that he stopped his truck and ran back to see if there was any thing he could do to help.

He said, "The man was hollering, 'Help, help, get me out of here!' I reached and got a hold of his hand and tried to pull him out, but I couldn't. Then there was an explosion!"

The gas had been leaking and exploded and he had to get back.

"I felt so bad, I just felt so horrible," he said.

What happened was; they were driving out in Arizona on a highway with wide shoulders, and one of those recaps was laying there in her lane, and when her headlights caught that, she darted over real quick to miss that recap tire, and ran right in front of this eighteen-wheeler that was going around them.

The truck driver said, "I couldn't do anything, but all I heard then was; he was quietly just worshiping Jesus."

He and two of their children died in that accident. His wife and oldest daughter were thrown away from the vehicle, and even though their clothes caught on fire, they lived.

Encouraging New Disciples

So God began to put it on our hearts to go see these disciples. We just kept feeling urged to go visit this work that our missionary friend started in Honduras.

Finally we just set a time, and said, "We're going."

So we went to Belize City, and caught an airplane over to Tegucigalpa, Honduras and from there we took a bus over the hill to the village where he had evangelized. On one side of this hill it was tropical, on the other side it was desert. It is amazing how that happens. Those people lived way back out in the desert. We caught this old rickety bus; and it took us several hours to finally get to this place. We had told the driver who we were coming to see and he stopped in front of the house. As we got off of the bus we saw about four or five men running toward us. They were really in a hurry to get there and fell on our necks and began to weep! We had never seen these people before we didn't know their names except the name of the one we were going to see, but they began weeping, and weeping. You could tell it wasn't a weeping of sorrow it was of joy. You can weep for joy too, can't you?

Finally they began to speak to us in Spanish and my brother was interpreting it into English so that I could understand too.

"We have been praying and praying for God to send somebody to teach us more in the Word of God," they said.

They had built a little church and reached out to other villages and started works all around there. They were brand new Christians but they wanted to know more, they were so hungry. When they told us this story we understood why they came weeping.

A few days before as they were praying and asking God for this teaching, God gave one of the young men a vision. In this vision he saw two men coming to teach them from God's Word. When we got off of the bus we were those two men, they recognized us! That's why they were so glad to see us and came weeping for joy. When you feel urged of God to do something, He has something in mind He wants to do. He just needs a vessel to work through.

When it came church time the women sat on one side and the men on the other.

"Just preach all night if you can," they said.

Now wouldn't that be something? They sat right on the edge of their seats and didn't miss a thing. You'd think they would get so full that they would want to go home and go to bed. No, not so. They gave us a little lean-to with a little straw mattress cot like thing where we could sleep. They would come and pack that little room out. They would ask questions until we would just fall asleep. When we could not stay awake any longer then they would go home. Before we could possibly get up the next morning here they were back again. That's how hungry they were. It just broke our hearts. I could see what our brother meant because the people we were staying with were so poor. They had a little baby, and that baby would drink donkey's milk. That's all they had. When the baby got hungry they milked the little donkey and fed the baby donkey's milk. Then I understood how blessed we are in this country and how often we grumble and complain. Oh, let's have a thankful heart.

We were there for several days and it was that way every day we were there. Then we went back home, just rejoicing in our hearts to know that God had answered these people's prayers, and used us to do it!

They were praying, "God send somebody to teach us more about Your Word."

Native Evangelists

So a few months later this same missionary friend from Mexico and I decided to go back to Honduras. There is a way that you could go by road, and we took a little '68 Ford pickup with a little box we built on the back and went over those mountain ranges. At that time El Salvador and Honduras had been fighting wars and we went through there where all the bullets had just riddled the buildings and everything else. We thanked the Lord for keeping us safe.

We got over there and the Lord put it on our hearts to take one of the brethren to Tegucigalpa and buy them a motorcycle. They had no means of transportation. They caught the old rickety bus to go to some places they wanted to go. Other times they would walk for miles to reach some of the more remote villages, just to tell people about Jesus. These were the natives there.

So we took him and bought the motorcycle, put it in the truck and took it back to their village. He had never ridden a motorcycle. So then we proceeded to teach him how to ride. He finally learned to ride well enough to get his license and drive it.

Then they said to us, "We would like for you to go to with us to this village but it is really difficult to get to. We can't even get a motorcycle in there. We will have to walk for miles back in there."

"Well, let's go," we said.

We drove as far as we could and left the old truck there and started down this trail going back to this village. We met many people coming out and they were carrying their tow sacks with their goods in them. They were in a hurry to get out of that village.

They were saying, "Oh don't go there. There's a family feud going on and people are shooting and killing each other. It's not safe back there, don't go!"

It wasn't just one or two; there were a lot of people coming out of there very fast.

So we stopped at a big rock bed there and prayed, "Lord, if you want us to go on into this village and help these people, we will go, but if You're telling us to turn back, we'll turn back."

Guess what the Lord said?

"Go!" He said.

When you say, "I'll go where You want me to go, dear Lord," that's not always easy; but He will be with you.

So we went on and kept meeting people in a hurry to leave.

"Oh, go back. Go back!" they would all tell us.

We got there and guns were going off all around us, and people were being killed. The Christian people were in the church and were really frightened, and didn't know quite what to do. They didn't know if they should leave or if they should stay. We were in the church with them and it gave them courage when we told them that God had sent us there.

Do you know what we began to do? We praised God, gave thanks to God, just lifted our hands and worshiped Jesus. In about an hour, maybe two, all of a sudden the guns stopped going off.

God is greater than the adversary. He's greater than the ones that come against us.

So what God wanted to do was strengthen the faith of those believers. They hadn't had an opportunity to learn and listen and gain knowledge, and all of those things like all of us have. So the Lord just wanted to show them that He was able to take care of them, and to believe what He said in His Word. If we will just believe, He'll do the rest.

A Blessing in Disguise

I had an old camper on the back of this pickup truck with a little bed in it; and when I could get to it, I liked to sleep in there. One night while sleeping in this camper, I felt the truck begin to rock.

I've been in campers on mountains in Arkansas where the hogs would come and scratch their backs under your truck, causing it to wobble.

"Boy, there must be some hog scratching his back on this truck," I thought.

I looked out the window. There was a house nearby and the shutters on the windows were just flopping back and forth.

"That's no hog scratching, that's an earthquake!" I said, "There's a bad earthquake somewhere."

We don't have many earthquakes in Belize. We have hurricanes, but not many earthquakes.

I found out the next morning on the news that the earthquake was in Guatemala. Guatemala borders Belize. Some of the Guatemalans have felt for many years that Belize really belonged to them, so they've tried in lots of ways to take Belize under their control.

Anyway, it just so happened that, not too long before that, we had brought back a big school bus loaded with clothes, blankets, shoes and things for the people in Belize.

I told the people loading the bus for Belize, "Don't put any heavy clothes in there because it never gets cold," but they did anyway; and the Lord knew why.

When the earthquake hit there wasn't a city in that part of Guatemala that wasn't affected by it. There was one Catholic Church that had walls 12 feet thick and it shook it plumb to the ground. There wasn't a family that wasn't affected by that earthquake.

We learned later that the Guatemalan army had made plans to invade Belize the next day. We learned that from one of the high ranking officers that we met at a Full Gospel Business Men's Meeting.

"We had our planes, tanks and solders ready to invade Belize; and that night is when the earthquake hit!" he told us.

They had something to think about instead of invading Belize. A lot of the Guatemalan people; Spanish people don't like the people of Belize, and we lived right on the main road just a few miles from the Guatemalan border, but they couldn't carry out their plan because the hand of the Lord stopped them.

So I was praying, "God, do you want us to go over to Guatemala, and take food, clothing and things over there? Do You want us to do that?" I asked.

Here is what He told me, "I didn't put that border between Belize and Guatemala that was man's doing. I love people no matter who they are or where they are. I supplied these goods for you--take them over there."

So the ladies took some of the very heavy clothes and made quilts and stuff out of them, and we loaded up our Ford pickup truck with the camper. We bought a few hundred pounds of beans and rice, and sacked them up into small portions.

A young minister from Belize went in my truck with me on that mission trip. I met one of the brothers we knew who lived just across the border, and he invited a Guatemalan Pastor to go with him in his vehicle.

He took his big bread type van loaded with clothing and stuff, and we all headed out to go do what we could to help the people.

We found some villages way back up in the mountains. He put his truck in low gear to make it up these mountains. Just narrow little trail roads to get up there, and way down there is the bottom. Of course our truck was four-wheel drive, so we made it.

Every day at evening time we would stop, have service and share Jesus. The people were so spiritually hungry. They were devastated. They needed God in their hearts. Many of them were Catholic, but religion doesn't cut it when you face death and all these things happen to you, and everything is taken away. You've got to have God. Religion just won't do it.

In the day time we would go through the villages and pass out clothes, food and stuff. We learned not to pass out anything going into the village, but wait until we were on our way out; because they would actually mob you, just for a pair of pants, shoes or food; they were desperate. So we would have services and then pass out the clothes and food.

When we would think we were way out in the boonies where nobody would find us, we'd stop and grab a whole bunch of stuff and put it up in the cab with us, and hardly before we could get back in the truck to go, the people would come running. If you didn't get away, you wouldn't get away, because they would surround the truck. They would follow us for miles just for a piece of clothing or a little bit of food. Like I said, when it would come evening time we wouldn't pass out any clothes or food, but we would first tell them about Jesus. Then when we would leave the next morning, we'd give them the clothes and food.

We learned as we went that you have to *"be wise as serpents and harmless as doves"* (Matt. 10:16 NKJV).

We would always go to the alcalde first. That's the main guy in the town like the mayor here, but they call them alcalde there. We would go to him and get permission to have service and tell them about Jesus.

After we had been in Guatemala a few nights we were having a service in this village. Right in the middle of the service these two jeeps full of Army officers drove up and arrested us! They had us pull our trucks into their military compound and locked us up, vehicles and all!

"You can't continue having meetings here!" they said.

The Guatemalan Pastor riding with the Guatemalan missionary said, "Let me go talk to them and see if I can get things right."

He went and talked to them and all he did was make it worse! He made those guys extremely angry.

Now, in Guatemala they can seize your vehicle without any kind of permission or anything else. They might seize it and everything you've got. So the Guatematlan brother was really shaken up.

I said to him, "Brother, they will not keep us here because I asked God if we were suppose to come here, and He said, 'Go!' So I know that the Lord is with us and they're not going to take our vehicles, and they are not going to keep us in here!"

We slept in our vehicles that night.

They came out the next morning and said, "We are going to let you go, but we are going to give you a command, 'Do not have any more services in Guatemala!'"

It reminded me of what they told the disciples in the Bible days, *"Don't preach or teach any more in that name"* (See Acts 4:18).

The Sadducees and others threatened Peter and John back then and these soldiers were threatening us! So we were in good company. We didn't have any more services there until the next night. The next night came and we went right on doing just exactly the same as we had been doing, because those people needed the comfort of the Holy Spirit. They needed to know who Jesus is. They needed to know that He loves and cares for them. Even though they had gone through this disaster they could find peace and comfort in knowing the Lord.

If we drove into a city of any size we would see people standing or sitting outside. They were not in their houses even if their house was still standing because they were afraid there would be more earthquakes. So they were living on the street under a piece of cardboard or a sheet or something. Disaster was everywhere you looked but yet their hearts were reaching out.

This is what the Lord is concerned about, that we reach out to the lost. That is why Jesus left Heaven and came to the earth, to seek and to save those that were lost. We saw God do many, many wonderful things.

A Trap Averted

We were coming home from a village way in the south of Belize one night. There was another couple with me in our van, and I was getting so sleepy. The services there don't get out at 7:30 or 8:00 o'clock. People aren't in a hurry to get there, but once they get there, they are not in a hurry to leave either. So the service had lasted until almost midnight and we had many, many miles to go over those rough roads. I got so sleepy; I could *not* keep my eyes open. The road was so rough and I was trying to dodge those chuck holes. You'd think you would never get sleepy, but when your body gets so tired your brain just wants some rest. So I pulled over to the side of the road and laid my head back against the seat, and slept for five minutes. After five minutes I woke up, felt refreshed, and was ready to go.

So we were driving along and the other couple was asleep. As I topped over a little hill and started down this little grade there was a man lying across the road. It looked like a drunk or a dead man lying in the middle of the road! This was not uncommon in Belize. I have gotten out many, many times, and moved a person that was drunk to the side of the road, to keep them from getting run over by another vehicle. So that is what I intended to do.

I had to almost pull up to the edge of the road. I pulled up to his feet and was getting ready to open the door to get out; when the Holy Spirit said, "Get out of here!"

You know, sometimes God speaks to us in a quiet, beautiful, soft voice, and other times it is more of a command and we need to obey.

"Get out of here!" He said.

So I didn't even question, I just put my foot on the accelerator and took off. As I went by I could see that it was a dummy that had been put there to trap me. If I had gotten out of the van, they would have had me; because as I took off, flashlights came on, on both sides of the road right behind me! They were just waiting to trap someone.

The enemy lays traps for us, but if we'll listen, the Holy Spirit will take us through; or lead us around. He knows exactly what is happening and how to take care of us.

The purpose of sharing the things in this book is to help people get to know who the Lord really is.

"[God is] a very present help in [every time of] trouble" (See, Ps. 46:1).

Whatever the need may be, He's there. He is always there. It's not just when we come to church and feel so good, praising God and shouting. Yes, He is there at that time and we thank God for that. I don't like to go to a church where the Lord is not there, do you? No, I'm spoiled; I want to see the Lord working and doing things and people responding to what God wants to do. God wants people to know who He really is. Who is He? He's not just a religion. He's not just a doctrine. He is life; and He is abundant life.

Wallet Lost

One day a young man and I decided to go up in the mountains of Arizona. We spent three days fasting and praying, and nothing else. We were just seeking the Lord. Many times I had gone up there, but this particular time we went up there together. In those three days neither one of us received any great revelation, or any great vision; nothing great happened. I've learned that it is not always in the time of fasting that you receive something. Many times God reveals something afterward.

Anyway, we came down from the mountain that evening. It was a church night that night, so my brother reached for his wallet, and he didn't have it.

"I have lost my wallet. I lost it up there somewhere," he said.

"Well, we'll just have to go back up there tomorrow and find it," I replied.

So the next day we got in the truck and drove back up there. We looked everywhere and couldn't find it. He would go one way and I'd go the other, while we were up there. I didn't know where all he went; but we retraced everywhere he thought he had been and we could not find that wallet.

We saw an old cave there that was actually a silver mine at one time. So we went in the mouth of that old cave and had a prayer meeting.

Yes, it had come to that! Sometimes we exhaust everything we know and finally decide to pray.

I don't feel like the Lord is angry with us because we don't come to Him first. I think He's just waiting for us to come, don't you? Do you think He knew where that wallet was? Absolutely!

A Word from God

So we began to pray in the mouth of that old cave.

"Lord, would you show us where the wallet is?" we asked.

We were talking to God about finding the wallet. The Lord never mentioned the wallet. This was one of the few times that the Lord ever spoke to me through my own mouth.

It was like a prophesy coming to me through my own mouth, and this is what the Lord was saying, "Be careful to exalt Me. Many are exalting doctrines about Me, but you be careful to exalt Me."

I can hear it just as plain right now as I did that day. That was the Word of the Lord that really did something in me. He's not just a doctrine. He is doctrine, yes, there is a doctrine, but He is more than that, He is life! It touched me then, and it still does.

He warned me and I have taken the warning, "Be careful to exalt Me."

This is one way that you can tell if something is true or false, any teaching, doctrine, or theory that does not exalt the Lord; is not of the Lord. He is not in the business of exalting man or our ideas. If it's of God, then it will exalt Him; and if it exalts Him, then He will back up His Word.

Wallet Found

The amazing thing was, after the Lord spoke this, we stayed there in His presence for some time. We just melted in His presence. When we walked out of that cave, there on a stump, lay his wallet! We had passed that stump on the way in and didn't see it. So him forgetting his wallet is what took us back up there to hear a powerful Word from God.

The reason I'm saying this, is to pass it on to all of us; let's be careful to exalt Him. Don't get so tied up in doctrines, people fall out over doctrines. They have misunderstandings, fall out of fellowship, quit going to church; and blame God for this that and the other. Let's exalt Him, and if we do, it will draw us together. It will bring us together because that is the Lord Himself and He is love. Praise God!

Chapter 9

His Present Help

Prayers Prayed

The Scripture says, *"Whatever things ye desire, when ye pray, believe that ye receive them, and ye shall have them"* (Mark 11:24). I believe that.

To me it's the top rung of the ladder when it talks about, *"Whosoever shall say unto this mountain, Be thou removed, and be thou cast into the sea; and shall not doubt in his heart, but shall believe that those things which he saith shall come to pass, he shall have whatever he saith"* (Mark 11:23).

Now a lot of times we look at that, and say, "But, I could never reach that."

Like the little woman that prayed for the mountain that obstructed her view of the sea to be moved.

She woke up the next morning and it was still there.

"Just as I thought, it's still there," she said.

Do you know why it wasn't moved? She didn't believe. If you had enough faith to move a mountain and cast it into the sea, that would be the top of the ladder. But you know, Jesus is so beautiful, He starts at the bottom rung with each one of us. There are many rungs in the ladder; it depends on how tall the ladder is.

Jacob saw a ladder that reached all the way into heaven. I'm on that ladder somewhere, aren't you? I'm somewhere on my way climbing up that ladder to heaven.

Jesus goes back and makes it so simple, and says, "Whatever things."

This means every day little things, big things, whatever things you desire; that is the key--desire. Not, I hope God will do it, maybe He will, I hope He does, but whatever you crave; you desire, when you pray.

What is prayer? It's talking to God. It's not just pretty words. It is manifesting your heart's desire in words to God. That's what prayer is. What I want to share with you now is an answered prayer.

What I want to share with you now is an answered prayer.

Do you believe God hears you when you pray? Or is it just certain people that He hears? Does He hear you? He hears you! He doesn't always answer immediately, but if you pray and believe, He will answer that prayer.

I want to tell you about a prayer that seemed to go unanswered; but God heard and answered.

Now, many times we make the mistake when we pray, to try to tell God how to do it. Then we are disappointed when He doesn't do it that way. So we think God didn't answer. But when we pray and believe God, then leave the way He's going to do it in His hands.

He said, *"if we ask anything according to His will, He hears us. And if we know that He hear us, whatever we ask,* [already have before we ever see] *we know that we have the petitions that we have asked of Him"* (1 John 5:14-15 NKJV).

So when we pray and believe, then we start thanking God for the answer. We start living in an expectancy to see how God is going to do this.

I had an uncle. My grandfather was a Minister, and that was his son. He grew up in church. He belonged to the First Pentecostal Church in Hot Springs, Arkansas. It was a big church; a lot of people went there. He married the Pastor's daughter, but World War 2 broke out; he was drafted, and sent overseas to fight against Japan. While he was gone his wife saw a young man she thought was a little bit better, so she left my uncle and married the other man.

This hurt him so bad that you could not talk to him about God. He thought religion was a fake, it was not real; and he lived that way for over forty years.

His mother, my grandmother, prayed for him. She prayed for him fervently until she died and no change. My dad and he were very close and Dad tried to talk to him about the Lord. My dad also prayed for him until he died; and no results. In fact, all of our family prayed for him to return to the Lord. It looked as if God didn't hear our prayers.

Sometimes we look at outward circumstances and say, "God didn't hear me."

But He did, He heard you.

My uncle and I became very close when he came back from the service. He became an airplane flight instructor teaching young GI's how to fly. I always liked to fly so we would go flying together. He was teaching me how to fly on the "GI Bill," even though I wasn't a GI. Sometimes some of the men wouldn't get the hours they needed in, so we'd fly on their time. So we became very close.

I'm telling you this to let you know how God answers prayer when you may think, "All hope is gone."

Many years had passed. We left the United States and went to Belize at God's bidding. We were there for a number of years and hadn't seen my uncle very much.

He worked for Trans World Airlines in later years, and became an inspector for Trans World Airlines. Then he retired from Trans World Airlines and became a Texas "Snowbird." He moved from up north down next to the border of Old Mexico.

His first wife had divorced him. In fact, he had been married five or six times.

You know, when you're miserable inside, it's hard to be a husband like you should be, so it just didn't work. My sister had written him a letter not too long before this incident that I'm going to tell you about, occurred.

She wanted to just reach out to him in love, and wrote, "You know, Uncle, we love you, and we're praying for you."

A lot of our family members considered him the black sheep of the family and just kind of turned their backs on him.

But she said in her letter to him, "I want you to know we love you and we are praying for you."

He answered her right back, "I'm glad you love me, but I don't need your prayers. Pray for somebody else, I don't need your prayers," he wrote.

That's the heart he had.

God was going to answer prayer, but not in any kind of way that we would have suspected or thought about.

Shopping Trip

There was a young man in Belize that had been under our ministry and God called him into the ministry. So he was also a Minister. He had a little saw mill way back in the woods in Belize and needed a logging skidder.

It rains a lot there, one hundred and eighty inches a year. If you don't have good equipment you can't get the logs out to the saw mill.

So he asked me if I would go with him to the United States and help him locate a good logging skidder. Then, of course, we would have to ship it back. I told him I would.

You know, when I'm traveling, I don't just travel, we are talking about the Lord, and we're in the Scriptures.

The men that God called into the ministry in Belize, we taught and trained them in duty. We would take them out working, ministering, sharing the Gospel, having meetings and all of those things. That's how we taught them. We would also train them to obey God. To let God move and watch God touch hearts.

So on this journey we just spent the time sharing Scriptures and things. We asked God to guide us, because this was a little bit out of my line. I'm not used to looking for logging skidders. So we ask God to guide us and He did. We found the skidder that he needed; took it to New Orleans, and made arrangements for the shipping company to ship it to Belize City, in Belize.

We had driven up to the States in this Ford van the Lord helped us get, which had a gasoline engine in it at first, but that engine had been removed and replaced with a diesel engine. Deisels are popular now, but they weren't back then. It was too far RPM's between some of the gears, so it needed another gear put in it. I was going to leave it until I got a six-speed transmission put in it, and then later take it back to Belize, but he decided he wanted to take some things down for his sawmill and some things for his family, and we needed that van to take all he wanted to take.

I really didn't want to take it, but he said, "We'll put the transmission in it later, we'll get it fixed, but we just need to take it now, to take all of this stuff."

Then we loaded that Ford deisel van with parts and equipment for the missionary work in Belize.

Now, all of this was God's doing. God is working many times when we don't even recognize what He is doing.

Arrested!

So we loaded it up with all this stuff and drove to the border. You never know what to expect when you get to the Mexican border. They make up their own laws as they go along.

We had all of our papers already done and were ready to go when this fellow came out to the van.

"You need to go with me to our Custom's Headquarters here in Matamoros and get a special permit to take some of the things you have in this van," he told us.

Of course none of the things were mine, they all belonged to the other missionary from Belize.

"Okay," I said.

So the border guard crawled in the van and directed us to their headquarters. When we got there they arrested us; both of us! They put us in this guard house. We could see out, but we couldn't get out. Those guards started unloading the van and taking everything they wanted!

They would put something to one side, and say, "That's mine; this is mine, this is mine..."

They took everything they wanted out of the van and it started to rain.

Then they told us, "Now, you can go out and put it back in."

So we went out in the cold rain and began putting the stuff back in the van that they hadn't taken.

How would you feel like when you've spent days shopping, trying to get this part, and that part, something here, and something there; have it all together in your van, and you've just watched them come and take what they wanted? You can't know unless something like that has happened to you.

Here's the whole point; God wants to give us the grace we need, when we need it; because if you don't have grace when you need it, you'll come unglued at the seams when something like that happens. You will get so mad and so vexed that the devil will just take you over. He will rob you of all your victory and faith. He'll make your mouth say things you did not want to say. He really will try and take over, but God's grace is sufficient.

So we went out there thinking, "Now maybe they're going to let us go, since they've taken all those things."

When we got what they had left back in the van, they put us back in the guard house. There we sat, hours are rocking by, when all of a sudden I became aware that something was wrong.

I turned to this brother, "They are going to put us in jail!" I exclaimed.

"Oh no, they wouldn't do that," he said.

"No, I know they are going to put us in jail," I replied.

Sure enough, about 10:00 o'clock that Saturday night, they came out, took me out behind the van; opened the doors and took pictures.

The next morning's paper came out, "Preachers, smugglers, tax evaders; running contraband."

That's what the paper said, and they wanted my picture in it. That wouldn't make you feel real good, would it?

Now, if you ever go to jail; don't go to jail in Mexico. It's not a place you would want your dog to be. It was actually horrible. It was filthy, and the food they served there was like slop, so I did not eat any. I remember they took us and closed the door behind us in that cell. The cell was made for about twenty-five or thirty people, and there were about fifty-five men in there.

There were people from the United States, Mexico, El Salvador, Honduras and many other countries; even Cuba, in that jail. It was the devil's den. I'll never forget when they closed the door what it felt like to be in the devil's den.

The devil came to me and said, "I've got you on my territory now, you're on my turf."

Do you want to make the devil mad? Go win souls. Go take the souls out of his snare which he intends for them to be in eternal destruction. If you really want to make him mad, just go win souls to Christ.

"I've got you on my territory now," he said.

And that's what it felt like! It felt like the devil's den. There were drug users, dealers; thieves, homosexuals and everything else in that cell.

It felt like, in the natural; "God, where are You? Have You forsaken me? Why am I here? All these charges they've put on me are false."

Of course these men had seen my picture and they were just laughing and making fun.

One guy from Cuba could speak English, and said, "They'll never believe you are a preacher, look at you."

It was just like the devil was laughing at me. But I want you to know, our God is real. This is not a religion, this is reality, and there's no place you can go that God won't be with you.

He said, "*I am with you always*" (Matt. 28:20).

So I'll never forget, I was in there, and the enemy began to say, "You'll never get out of here."

All of those men were telling me. "You have broken the laws that are really so important to Mexico. If you would have killed somebody, it wouldn't have been as bad as running contraband, tax evasion, and smuggling."

Especially the tax evasion charge because they're looking for the dollar.

"You will never get out of here," they said.

I confessed, while I was feeling the lowest, "I will *not* be here long, because this is not where God called me. I know He called me to Belize. He didn't say anything about the Mexican jail, so I won't be here long!"

Now, I was confessing that to them, but I was also confessing it to myself! In my heart I knew I would not be there long.

"Uh-huh, this 'gringo' doesn't know what he's talking about," they said.

Many of them had been in there for many, many years, and could not get out.

When I told them, "I'm not going to be here long," they just laughed at me.

After I was there a few days, I understood why they laughed; because you just didn't get out. You can get in, but you can't get out!

So the first night I spent fighting with the devil. I hardly got any sleep in there anyway because there were twice as many men as there were bunks.

Revival in Jail

On Sunday afternoon, my second day there, our representative in Mexico who was suppose to be an American consul for people in trouble, came to my cell, at my request.

He listened to me, "I'm sorry, there's nothing I can do to help you," he said.

"What are we paying you for? You are supposed to help Americans who get in trouble. These charges are false. If there was something in my van at the border that shouldn't be there they would have turned us back. Don't you see this was a setup?" I reasoned.

It was really a setup by God, but He used the devil to bring it to pass. Do you know that the devil is God's little devil? He does a lot of things he wished he wouldn't have done later. He crucified Jesus for one, and then wished he wouldn't have done it.

He has touched God's people all down through the ages, and when it's all over, he says, "I wished I'd have left them alone."

God was working on their behalf then and He works on our behalf now. He is the same God, He's our God.

Anytime the devil touches you and God works for you; he will say, "I wish I would have left them alone. All I did was bring them a brand new testimony. Now they can share that, and it will touch other people."

Later that evening I was really feeling in my heart; I just wanted some "alone time" with the Lord. Where was I going to get that? There was no bush to get behind, there was no way to get away from anybody. I mean, people were packed in that cell.

Over in the corner was an old guitar. It looked like it was the first thing off of Noah's ark. It was beat up, oh my goodness; it wouldn't bring fifty cents here in the States; but there it was. I don't know how it got there; because they would not even let me take my razor, change of clothes or anything into that cell. God must have planted it there.

I saw this old guitar, and asked, "Who does this belong to?"

"Just play it, go ahead and play it," somebody said.

So I crawled up on the top bunk, leaned back against the wall, and started strumming on that old guitar.

David said, *"Thou preparest a table before me in the presence of mine enemies"* (Ps. 23:5).

Let me tell you, these Scriptures that we read, are so precious, but when we get in certain circumstances, they become a whole lot more precious.

"Lord I'm here, in the devil's den, but You are with me. You said You would be with me," I said.

I closed my eyes and started worshipping the Lord and strumming that old guitar. I don't know how long I played that old guitar because I lost track of time, but I was in God's presence. Do you know all fear left? There's no fear in the presence of Christ. The fear was gone. I knew I was in God's hands, and I was just worshipping the Lord in song.

Then eventually, I became aware of the fact that you could hear a pin drop in that cell. I opened my eyes and peaked out and every eye in that cell was glued on me up on that top bunk. The presence of God arrested those men; just His presence. There was no whooping and hollering and shouting. I believe in all of that, but sometimes; just His presence--His very real presence will flood a place. God turned that devil's den into a place of revival!

When God's presence came in, it overruled all of those things. The next thing you know, many, many of those men were on their knees, on that cold, filthy, cement floor; crying, praying, and asking God to forgive them!

The ones that had laughed at me, and said, "You're not going to get out of here, look at you; a preacher, breaking all of these laws," were among them.

The next day each one of them would come, and they all said the same thing: "God sent you here just for me."

"It must have been, because I would not have come here on my own, I guarantee you," was my answer.

I would *not* have gone there on my own.

They began to tell me, "I have a praying mother, grandmother, aunt or wife."

Who ever they knew that had been praying for them. God was answering those prayers that had been sent up to Him; petitioning Him. He was using me to answer their prayers, and I didn't know that. God is faithful. He has ways of doing things that are way past our understanding. It just blessed me so much I didn't even care if I was in jail anymore! To reach out and see souls being born again, right there in the devil's den; right in his face, made it worth it all.

When Satan makes his boast, and says, "I've got you now, I've got you now."

You can say, "No you haven't, you've just given me a brand new testimony!"

Now we like the testimony but the test is not always easy, and if we could, we would leave off the test, and just have the "mony." But God wants to give us a testimony of His love and of His reality, that no matter where we are, He is with us.

"If God be for us, who can be against us?" (Rom. 8:31).

Becoming a Pastor

There was one little man in there from El Salvador. He was the only Christian in that cell. He had practically memorized the whole New Testament. God was setting the stage. He had prepared a Pastor before revival ever broke out. They had laughed and made fun of him, but when God moves me on he was going to be their Pastor. He got so happy; he would just laugh, and then he'd cry.

He would laugh and say, "Oh Brother, I'm so glad you're in here, I haven't had any fellowship in years." He was so blessed, and then he'd cry, and say, "But I'm so sorry to see you in a place like this."

The Chief of Police of Matamoros came into the cell two or three times and visited with me.

"I know you don't belong in here," he said.

The Lord caused him to know that. He didn't know me from anybody, but he just knew that.

"I wish there was something I could do to help you, but this is a Federal offense, and I can't do anything," he said.

But I said, *"The Lord is my helper"* (Heb. 13:6).

I don't have any way of knowing what happened to all those different men that accepted Christ because I had no way of keeping track of them, but I know I'll meet many of them; if not all of them, when we reach the other shore. That knowledge was such a joy in my heart. Then when they came to know Christ we were constantly sharing with them. So we had continual revival in there.

After four days the guards came and took me and some others to another jail there in the same town. That was the year that all the fruit trees in southern Texas froze and there was no heat of any kind in those cells; nothing. In fact, the Belizean brother I was with developed pneumonia in there because of the cold and the conditions.

We were already about freezing to death and they moved us in the back of an old pickup truck; and put us in that other cell. The reason this happened was because God had some other people He wanted to reach.

God hears our prayers. And if He has to send missionaries from Belize falsely accuse them, and put them in jail, he'll get those who have been prayed for. God will reach them. Be faithful to pray and believe God.

Pray for your family members and those who have never been able to be reached. Pray for them; because God will reach them. He does answer prayer.

Some Heat Provided

When we were taken to that other cell I learned that the District Attorney's office was on the floor above us. The Chief of Police came to see me again in that cell.

"I wish there was something I could do for you," he said.

Up to this time I hadn't eaten anything, taken a shower, or been able to shave.

"Let me ask just one request. I believe there are offices upstairs, is that correct?" I asked.

"Yes," he replied.

"Don't they close about nine o'clock?" I asked.

"Yes they do," he answered.

"Would they happen to have a little electric heater in one of those offices that you could bring down and put in our cell when they close?" I asked.

"I can do that," he said.

Later he brought in one little heater. There were about 15 to 20 men in this second cell. We took turns backing up to that one little heater and getting a little warmth.

The guards would come in and take some man out and you could hear him screaming as they beat him until he confessed to whatever they wanted him to say. They did that with several of the men. It was horrible. The Lord never allowed them to take me out and beat me, but it hurt me so bad to hear the others being treated that way. There was an older gentleman that was taken out and never came back to the cell. I guess they beat him to death!

Bad Interpretation

Three days after being moved to the other cell, it came my time to be called before the District Attorney upstairs. They don't have trials and things like we have here. They listen to your case and decide what they're going to do with you; and that's it.

So they came about 9:30 on a Friday night, and said, "The District Attorney wants to see you upstairs," and they escorted me upstairs.

I know just enough Spanish to get in trouble, so I requested an interpreter, because the D.A. wanted to know what happened at the border? What took place up there? Why am I here? What charges were laid against me, and how they came about? I began to speak to him and tell him exactly what took place.

"Actually, we were conned. We were just told that we needed to go to another location and get a special permit to take these things through for him across Mexico to Belize, Central America. Then when we got to the other location they arrested us and took whatever they wanted," I said.

As I was explaining all of this to him there was something inside me that knew this interpreter was not telling the District Attorney what I was saying! I knew a little Spanish. I didn't know enough to understand everything he was saying, but I knew he wasn't saying the same thing I was. I was watching the District Attorney's face and he was getting very angry. Did you ever see somebody get angry, and then angrier, and a little bit angrier? I knew by looking at that

District Attorney that I was just about to the point where I was going to be crucified!

Surprise Visitors

I cried out in my heart. I never said a word; nothing came out of my mouth, but in my heart, I cried, "Oh God, help me, I can't help myself!"

Just about the time I got through saying that, in my heart, there was a knock on the door to this District Attorney's office. The fellow that was interpreting for me went over there and opened the door. There stood my uncle; who didn't want anything to do with God, and his wife! To tell you the truth, I was totally shocked. Now if Jesus would have been standing there, I wouldn't have been surprised; but this uncle standing there was very shocking to me! How did he get there? How did he know about me? He and his wife that I had never met, was now standing outside the D.A.'s office door!

She was Spanish, born and raised in Mexico. He had met her over on the Texas side, and married her. I didn't even know he lived in that area, and there they stood!

It took me about a few seconds to come to myself, and I just ran and grabbed him and hugged him. Oh my goodness! Oh what a sight to see! The introductions were very fast because I knew I didn't have much time to say anything. I could tell by one look that his wife was Spanish.

"Would you interpret for me?" I pleaded, "Because this fellow that is interpreting for me is not telling the D.A. what I am saying."

"I will be glad to if the District Attorney will let me," she replied.

So they came into the office, and she introduced herself to the District Attorney. It turned out that her father had been a custom's officer on that border for twenty years; and had recently passed away. This District Attorney knew him well, and he was highly respected.

Let me tell you, when the devil thinks he's got you, God always has a way out!

The Spanish are very family orientated; they are very close, and I appreciate that about them. Although she had never met me, I was the nephew of her husband and she took me in as family.

So when the D.A. found out who she was, she asked him, "He's in my family, he is trying to explain to you what happened. Would you allow me to interpret for him?"

The District Attorney answered, "Sure, of course."

Well, the devil's agent that had intended to get me crucified; whoosh—he was gone. When God comes in the devil has to go! He can't stay around.

So we began at the beginning again, and explained to him what happened at the border.

"Well, I can see through things now," he said.

They took me and put me back in the cell and my uncle and his wife went home. They lived about sixty miles from there, in Mission, Texas.

Joy Explained

My uncle told this to me later.

"On the way home my wife began to cry. 'What's wrong, honey?' I asked her. 'I just can't stand to see the condition that Samuel is in, in that jail,' then she asked me, 'but why is he so happy?' I sat there for a minute thinking about it, and finally I had to say, 'He's happy because he's got the real thing!'"

She couldn't understand why I was so happy. I was happy because God was with me. When I cried out, He answered. He had saved souls. We were watching God at work. Why shouldn't I be happy?

One More Taunt

They took me and put me back in the cell; and a little while later, they came and opened the door; and said, "You are free to go!"

Those guys, who had made fun of me and said that I would never get out of that place, now couldn't believe their eyes. They were totally in shock!

I had told them, "I won't be here long."

I'm not saying anything about me, but they knew they had been visited by the Supreme God, the God of the entire Universe. God had been there and they knew He had been there. He had touched their lives in so many ways.

When they opened the door to let me out, the devil had one last thing, to taunt me with. He is a liar, but if he can get you to believe him, he will come and put fear in your heart. Now, I had seen many things go on while I was there. I was there exactly one week. Many terrible things had been done by those guards and I knew anything was possible; they were "crazy."

"Uh-huh, they're going to open the door and let you out; then they will say you are trying to escape, and they will shoot you!" the devil said.

Do you know what I did? I just laughed at him; I'm telling you the truth.

"Thank you, Mr. Devil, that's just a shortcut to Glory!" I said.

He couldn't get me; he couldn't put fear in my heart. "Just a short cut to Glory."

God takes away the fear, the fear of man, the fear of death and the fear of what people think.

He just moves that all out, and gives you that glorious sweetness of His love and presence, and says, "I'm with you, I am always with you."

Freedom!

I ran all the way back to the border and across that bridge, there wasn't another soul on the road anywhere.

When I crossed back, into this beautiful, wonderful country of the United States of America, I wanted to shout, "It's so good to be back in this wonderful country!"

But I didn't dare, because the way I looked and the way I smelled; I was afraid the U.S. authorities might decide, "There's something wrong with this guy, we'd better take him in for questioning."

So I quietly came back, and then ran to find a place to stay. About three or four blocks down the highway, I found a little cheap motel on the side of the road. I had a twenty dollar bill in my shoe they never found. So I took that and rented this room.

The first place I headed for was the shower. I washed out all of my underclothes, and hung them up. Then I turned that water on as hot as I could stand it. Oh, it felt so good. I didn't know a shower could feel so good! Not just to get the dirt off, but to warm my body up. When I got out of the shower, my undies weren't dry yet, so I just put on my pants and shirt and walked to a little restaurant they had connected with the motel, and got a hot bowl of soup. I hadn't eaten for a week. I never knew soup could taste so good; oh, my.

While I was sitting there eating this bowl of soup, there was a couple of senior ladies sitting at the table near me, and they were grumbling and complaining about having a flat tire.

I thought, "Ladies, if you only knew what a blessing it is to be where you could have a flat tire." Then later I prayed, "God, if I ever grumble about anything else again, remind me of that Mexican jail."

You would give anything to be where you could have a flat tire! I never knew just how wonderful freedom was until that day.

So I went back to my room. The next morning, I got on the phone; and called my uncle.

I said, "Uncle, guess where I am?"

When I told him, he said, "I'll be there as quick as I can get there."

This was a Sunday morning. He came and brought me a nice suit a white shirt, some clean underwear, and all of that. We were pretty close to the same size. So I shaved and changed clothes. Do you know what we did? We headed back across the border to go to the jail and get my friend from Belize out.

Some people might ask, "Weren't you afraid to go back over there?"

No. After I had cleaned up, shaved and changed clothes they didn't even recognize me.

My friend was so afraid, "Well, you're an American, that's why you got out," he said.

"No, that had nothing to do with it. It is not our nationality. It is because of who we are in Christ. Whatever nationality, whatever color, whatever race, it doesn't matter; it's our relationship with the Lord," I told him.

He said, "I probably won't ever get out of here. I'm going to loose everything I've got." Then he asked me, "Will you please take care of my family?"

"Oh, Brother, that goes without saying; you know me. You know I will take care of whoever I need to take care of, but you are going to get out too," I said.

I had to believe for me and him both.

On Monday afternoon they released him into my custody to leave the jail and go back to Belize! That's our God!

After we got out, my new found aunt said, "I have a real good friend just across the Mexican border in another town.

He has been our Attorney for years, and he's one of the best in Mexico. You've been conned, they took your van and everything, and we'll get it back."

I said, "Ok, we'll go see him."

So we went and told him the story, and he confirmed what I had said, that we had been conned. But by now, I was really glad that

I was conned; because my desire is to see souls saved. That's what God saved me for, to reach out to somebody else.

So after we talked to him he said, "I'll get the van back for you. You don't need to worry, I'll get it back; but if I don't get it back, it won't cost you anything."

I signed over power of attorney for my uncle to sign anything that would require my signature concerning the van, and any of our things they might be able to recover. Then since we didn't have anything to take back with us, we flew to Belize.

Good News and Bad

After we were back in Belize for about two weeks, I received a letter from this uncle. His letter read, "I have good news, and bad news. I'll tell you the good news first.

After you left, my wife and I said, 'We've got to get in church,' and we began visiting different churches."

You know people are looking for reality; they're looking for something real. Not just another religion, but some place where God is.

The letter continued, "We visited three or four churches, and couldn't find any that have what you have. We wanted what you have."

What did I have? I had the reality of a living God in me and working through me. I'm no special anybody just His servant, but He lives in me and He lives in you; if you are born again of His Spirit. That's what makes us special, we are special to God; and He is special to us.

The letter went on, "We found this little Assembly of God church and when we went in, we knew that was it. The second time we visited that church we both knelt at the altar and gave our hearts to God! That's the good news. Now for the bad news, the Judge wanted your van, and we couldn't get it away from him."

I started praising God!

"That van was to be used for winning souls, and it's already done its job," I thought.

There are many more vans out there. I didn't let the news that I didn't get my van back; dampen the good news about my uncle and his wife. They were born again! Her Mother and sister came into the body of Christ. Her three children also got saved and two of them are missionaries!

Don't give up. God answers prayer! No matter how He does it or who He uses, or what He does; He will find a way. If we don't give up, God won't give up; so don't give up.

Chapter 10

Walking on with Jesus

[botanical sprig decoration]

The Right Attitude

This brother and I were going together from Arizona back to Arkansas. Somewhere along the line, we were on a four-lane divided highway, and then it was a two-lane road, then it was a four-lane again. They were doing construction. We were just sharing and talking about the things of God like two brothers would together, and I didn't realize at that moment that I was in the left lane on a two-lane road! We were between Lordsburg and Deming, New Mexico.

Then I saw an eighteen-wheeler coming around a slight curve in my lane!

"What in the world is he doing in my lane?" was my first thought. My next thought was, "I don't care what he's doing in my lane; I'm getting over here!"

So I got back over because I had passed a vehicle and was waiting to pass another one; you know how you do on the freeway, and

I didn't realize that I was driving on the wrong side of the road! On a divided four-lane highway that would have been all right, but not on this two-lane highway.

There was a Highway Patrol following this eighteen-wheeler, and as we went by I saw him there, and said, "Uh-oh."

Sure enough, he made a U-turn and turned his lights on. I just pulled over, stopped and waited. He came up there, and I went back to talk to him, and he was writing me out a ticket! I was trying to talk to him to explain what happened on that freeway, and he would *not* listen to me at all!

So I began to get onto myself, "What a foolish stunt, of all the times you have driven all over the United States and different places; why would you pull such a crazy stunt like this?"

He charged me with driving on the wrong side of the road, no explanation; and almost causing a head-on collision. He would not listen or let me explain what had taken place.

So I went back and got in the pickup truck, and the brother asked, "Well, did he give you a ticket?"

I replied, "Yes he did."

I was upset at myself, and at him, because he wouldn't listen to me. I got real angry at myself and all of a sudden it seemed like out of now where, the Word of the Lord came to me. It was Romans 8:28 *"And we know that all things work together for good to them that love God, to them who are the called according to His purpose."*

That Scripture transformed my whole attitude. It did something inside of me because the first three words of that verse are very important; we've got to know that. *"And we know"* If you know, then you know; but if you just think you know, then you don't really know, do you? That Scripture was birthed in me that day, and all of a sudden, the whole atmosphere changed.

I said, "Thank you Lord, I'm going to witness to the Judge about You today."

Because the Patrolman said, "You've got to go to the next town, which is Deming; and you've got to stop and see the Judge; because you are out of state, and if you don't stop and see him, we'll arrest you."

So I said, "Thank you Lord, I'm going to testify to the Judge, and tell this Judge that we're all going to stand before the 'Great Judge' one of these days."

I felt good inside now. I'm excited and can hardly wait to see the Judge.

So we got to Deming and went to the Court House. We found the Judge's office, and went in to see the Judge.

A lady came to the door, I thought it was his secretary, and she said, "I'm the Judge."

Well I wasn't really prepared for that because I had never met a woman Judge before and it kind of took me by surprise.

She said, "Come on in, I'm expecting you, the Patrolman has already called in and told me about you."

So I went in and she sat behind her big desk and asked me if I'd like to be seated. Since we had been sitting for quite some time, I said, "I would rather stand, if you don't mind."

I asked her, "Would you let me explain to you what happened out there on the highway?"

Then I told her that we are on our way back to Arkansas to have some meetings and such.

"Yes, you can explain it to me, but I want to tell you that I've had lying preachers tell me lies to save their own skin," she replied.

Now listen, that was where the weak spot and sore spot was in me, because I had traveled all my life, and I had seen some pretty sneaky Pastors, preachers, and people who claimed to have God, pull crooked things.

This is why I had told the Lord, "I never, ever want to be a preacher!"

I just didn't want to be identified with that profession. There was bitterness in me. If God wouldn't have touched me on the road, this problem would not have been solved because her statement would have made me so angry.

But I thought, "Jesus, thank you for healing my heart, and for giving me the right attitude."

The Right Witness

So I asked her, "Do you believe in prayer?"

"Yes, I'm a Baptist, I pray every day," she answered.

"Would you let me pray, and ask God, call Him as my witness; that what I have told you is the truth?" I asked.

Because, I had explained to her what happened there. Isn't it wonderful to walk in the favor of God, tell the truth, and call Him as your witness?

"Yes, you may do that," she answered.

So I began to pray.

I just talked to God, and said, "Now Father, you know exactly what happened out on that road, and You know if I have told this lady the truth. If I've told her the truth, would You just bear witness to her heart that I have told her the truth?"

When I got through praying, she had her hankie out wiping her eyes; and said, "I believe--I believe you told me the truth."

"How do you plead, guilty or not guilty?" she asked.

"Well, I don't want to plead guilty!" I answered.

"If you don't plead guilty then you have to be here at a certain date and you will have to stand in court and all that," she said.

"Well, I will gladly do that," I said.

I'm feeling good, now see. When you're in the presence of God I don't care where it is, you feel good.

She said, "This is the date you will have to be here."

"Well, I can't be here, because I'm already scheduled to be in meetings in Arkansas on that date," I told her.

"You'll just have to plead guilty then, and pay the fine," she said.

He had charged me with driving on the wrong side of the road, and almost causing a head-on collision. This was a very serious charge, and it could have amounted to a lot of money.

"I have to charge you something, but what I'm going to do for you is charge you the bare minimum, which will cost you fifteen dollars," she said.

"Thank you, I appreciate that," I said.

I got my money out, and she was writing out the receipt and everything. When she handed me the receipt, she handed me a ten dollar bill back!

"I want to have a part in your ministry," she said.

It had changed from a lying preacher, to wanting to have a part in my ministry! That's when we call God as our witness. I'm talking about reality; calling God as our witness.

A Hungry Lamb

So I asked her, "Could we pray with you again?"

"I wish you would," she answered.

So we began to pray again, "Father; here is an honest Judge, that wants to Judge rightly. Would You give her that same wisdom that you gave Solomon, to be able to judge righteous judgment, what is right and what is wrong?"

We prayed, and blessed her; and again, the hankie was out and the tears were flowing. The presence of God will melt the hardest heart. It will melt the heart of those Judges who've got such a hard heart. However, this Judge was not one of those.

So we finally got through praying, and blessed her, and the other brother went out to the truck.

As I started out the door, she inquired, "Could you wait just a few more minutes?"

"Sure," I said.

And that hungry "little lamb" began to ask me questions about the Holy Ghost. I stood there for one solid hour ministering to that lady. Then I knew why the patrolman wouldn't listen to me on the road. I knew why, because God had a hungry "little lamb" He wanted to feed along the way. We know that all things work together for our good, because God sees fit that it will work together. I left there knowing that the Lord had done this. This was a setup by the Lord, to feed her hungry heart.

Questions Get Answered

Driving down the road my thoughts were, I didn't actually want to go ministering to these people, because they all had different doctrines, and different beliefs. I don't like to offend people. If God puts something on my heart I'll share it, but I don't like to just get up, and preach at this one, and preach at that one; like some preachers do. I just like to share what Jesus wants to do for each heart.

Praying as I went, "Lord, there's nothing I could preach that wouldn't cross somebody's doctrine here."

The Lord spoke to me and said, "Don't study for a sermon, just spend time with Me and in My Word, and I will give you what to say."

Now, this was a new step for me. I was going where people had been calling and calling, wanting me to come and now they were all expecting me to be there.

When I got there I saw that they had this big beautiful home, and it was filled upstairs, downstairs and everywhere with people. A lot of people, and when I looked at them, I thought of hungry little birds with their mouths open, waiting for their next meal. They were so anxious to hear what I had to say, and I didn't have anything to say. God didn't quicken one Scripture, one thought, or anything to me; and I am shaking. I don't know what to do.

"Lord, if you don't give me something, I'm going to tell the people it's Your fault," I thought.

That's right; because I had done exactly what He told me to do.

The Lord said, "I want to do this, I just need your mouth. Can I use your mouth?"

"Yes Lord, yes You can use me, Jesus," I answered.

I remember, there was only one place left for me to stand and that was over behind a recliner in the corner of the living room. I'll never forget when I stood up behind that recliner, the presence of the Lord came on me like a mantle and God's message just began to flow. I looked at those people up the stairs, down the stairs, in the dining room, the living room, everywhere; and I could literally see little question marks above their heads. Little question marks all over the place had appeared right above their heads! As the Spirit was working and speaking, I would see those little question marks just disappear. They began to disappear off of this one, off of that one, then off of the next one.

We saw this happen night, after night, and God began a strong work in those people. It was the Lord that did it. It all started back there on the road when I got the ticket; God had to work on me first.

He is preparing vessels that He can use in these last days. God has great things in mind for these days, and He has chosen us. This is our day to carry the torch, to be the light in this world. I just want to encourage you; don't take any thought when you meet somebody, what you're going to tell them. Just let the Holy Spirit minister, that's what He put the Holy Spirit in us for.

He said, *"I'll give you in that moment what you ought to say"* (See Matt. 10:19 & Mark 13:11).

So be led by God's Spirit.

Obedience Brings Results

Many years ago we were in a camp meeting in the Big Bear Mountains of southern California. We were there in a convention and many people were in attendance. The building was crowded and this *starchy* Englishman got up on the platform.

The way he was dressed, I thought; "If he would move just a little bit, he'd crack."

I mean, he was really spiffed up.

He stood up, and in his heavy British accent, said, "I have the oddest feeling--I feel like dancing."

There wasn't anything really going on to dance about, but he said, "That's why it felt odd, you know. I have the oddest feeling, I feel like dancing."

Then this senior English gentleman began to dance. There was a couple sitting in front of me that had differences they just couldn't seem to resolve, and they were looking at maybe having to get a divorce; but they decided they would go to this camp meeting first, and see if God would do something. When this older Englishman began to dance, other people began to dance, and this man's wife began to dance. This man was holding onto the seat in front of him, and was determined he was *not* going to dance. There wasn't even any music playing. Finally he turned loose and danced too! God healed their marriage! They didn't need that divorce. Hallelujah!

When you feel like obeying God, just obey God. There was a woman that had been rolled in, in a wheelchair, and sat over to the side there, and while everybody else was dancing; she decided she wanted to dance too. So she jumped out of the wheelchair and God healed her! Praise God!

We were camped out there, and after the meeting was over, this preacher came over to me, and inquired, "Brother Samuel, do think all that noise and carrying on in there was really of God?"

I answered, "You know what, that's not fair to ask me that question, why don't you ask the woman that was in the wheelchair?"

Let her testify. When God is in a thing, He fixes it right. So if you're having marriage problems, maybe you just need to dance a little bit. Get in the Spirit, praise God, worship God; in His presence is fullness of joy!

Solid Ground

In every testimony there is a test, but after the test, is a testimony. Now, I don't know about you, but I've failed a few tests. I didn't glorify God in the test. I grumbled and complained; why did God let this happen, and all this kind of thing.

When it was all over, and I saw that God was in it, I said, "God, forgive me, I don't want to go through that again."

If you fail a test, most of the time you take it again. You don't skip any grades in God. He wants the ground under us to be solid, when you say something, that's the way it is.

Walmart Gift

The other day I kept feeling like there was something God wanted me to do, but I really didn't have the finances to do it. But if God wants you to do something He will make a way. This wasn't a happenstance, God had a setup. I went to Walmart to get some diesel in my old truck, and there on the ground, lay what I thought was a piece of trash. When I picked it up and looked at it, it was a Walmart gift card.

"Somebody just used it up and threw it on the ground," I thought, "The trash can was right there, why didn't they put it in the trash?"

That's the way we are, we're kind of critical sometimes, but the Lord is not.

So I almost walked over and put it in the trash can, and I thought, "No wait a minute; just let me take it home, it might have something on it, at least a dollar or two."

So we took it home, checked it out and called the number. It had $291.16 left on it! If it had been a credit card, we could have run a check and found out whose it was, but it was a gift card. Somebody had already paid for that last Christmas. Somebody had given a gift card, we don't know who, but it was for $300.00, and all they spent from Christmas till now; left a balance $291.16! They had been saving that for me all that time, and didn't know it; but God knew it. Those things are not a happenstance. They aren't just something that happens, but God sets the course. From last December He set the course and made a way for me to do what He wanted me to do! So the Lord will be glorified and we will keep on keeping on for Jesus. I will not be denied, till Jesus comes and makes me whole. Hallelujah!

CPSIA information can be obtained
at www.ICGtesting.com
Printed in the USA
JSHW012140210922
30775JS00001B/6